**Nuclear
Weapons
in Europe**

Nuclear Weapons in Europe

Modernization and Limitation

Edited by
Marsha McGraw Olive
Jeffrey D. Porro
The Arms Control Association

WITHDRAWN

LexingtonBooks
D.C. Heath and Company
Lexington, Massachusetts
Toronto

Library of Congress Cataloging in Publication Data
Main entry under title:

Nuclear weapons in Europe.

   Bibliography: p.
   Includes index.
   1. Europe—Defenses—Addresses, essays, lectures. 2. Atomic weapons—Addresses, essays, lectures. 3. Atomic weapons and disarmament—Addresses, essays, lectures. I. Olive, Marsha McGraw. II. Porro, Jeffrey D.
UA646.N8   1982   355'.03304   82-47854
ISBN 0-669-05655-3

Copyright © 1983 by D.C. Heath and Company

All rights reserved. No part of this publication may be reproduced or transmitted in any form or by any means, electronic or mechanical, including photocopy, recording, or any information storage or retrieval system, without permission in writing from the publisher.

Second printing, June 1983

Published simultaneously in Canada

Printed in the United States of America

International Standard Book Number: 0-669-05655-3

Library of Congress Catalog Card Number: 82-47854

Contents

	Figures and Tables	vii
	Foreword *Gerard C. Smith*	viii
	Acknowledgments	xi
	Introduction	xii
Chapter 1	Nuclear Weapons in Europe: Perspectives on Negotiations *Elliot L. Richardson* and *Henri Simonet*	1
Chapter 2	Military Factors in Europe *Ivan Selin*	13
Chapter 3	Allies, Angst, and Arms Control: New Troubles for an Old Partnership *Josef Joffe*	21
Chapter 4	Long-Range-Theater Nuclear Forces in Europe: The Primacy of Politics *Andrew J. Pierre*	39
Chapter 5	Security Policy and Arms Control: A European Perspective *Klaas G. de Vries*	51
Chapter 6	Prospects for Limiting Nuclear Forces in Europe *Jane M.O. Sharp*	65
Chapter 7	Intermediate-Nuclear-Force Negotiations: Issues and Alternatives *Gregory F. Treverton*	81
Chapter 8	The Atlantic Alliance: Summing Up *Peter Corterier*	103
Chapter 9	NATO and Nuclear Deterrence *Richard Burt*	109
Appendix A	Chronology	121
Appendix B	NATO Communique, December 12, 1979	131
Appendix C	NATO Communique, December 14, 1979	135

Glossary	143
Bibliography	149
Index	161
About the Contributors	165
About the Editors	168

Figures and Tables

Figures

1–1	Major Intermediate-Range Nuclear Weapons Deployments in Europe	4
3–1	The Pershing II	28
3–2	Ground-Launched Cruise Missile	30
3–3	Pershing II and Pershing I Compared	32
4–1	A–7 Aircraft	43
4–2	FB–111A Bomber Launching a Short-Range Attack Missile	49
7–1	Soviet SS–4 Missile	82
7–2	Soviet SS–5 Missile	83
7–3	Soviet SS–20 Missile	84
7–4	Soviet Backfire Bomber	92
9–1	Pershing II and GLCM	115

Tables

6–1	U.S. and USSR Views of the Nuclear Balance	68
6–2	IRBMs and Medium-Range Nuclear-Capable Aircraft	69
6–3	Short-Range Nuclear-Capable Strike Aircraft	69
6–4	Tactical Nuclear-Delivery Vehicles	70

Foreword

In September 1981, the Arms Control Association—with the assistance of the NATO Information Directorate, the Royal Institute of International Relations (Brussels), and private West European and North American foundations—sponsored a conference in Brussels on the modernization and limitation of nuclear weapons in Europe. The aim of the conference was threefold: to examine East-West intermediate-nuclear-force modernization in the light of the military balance in Europe, to explore options to NATO for intermediate-nuclear-force (INF) negotiations, and to review the political climate influencing the range of INF choices, with a view to fostering better understanding among the NATO allies.

The conference was chaired jointly by Ambassador Elliot Richardson and Professor Henri Simonet, the former Belgian foreign minister. The participants included twenty-four specialists on political and security affairs from eight NATO countries and represented a spectrum of views on the intermediate-nuclear force issue (the term intermediate-nuclear force, or INF, has tended to replace long-range-theater nuclear forces, or LRTNF). After briefings from NATO officials, including Secretary General Luns, the participants focused their discussions on four conference papers. At special plenary sessions, the participants heard addresses from two key alliance officials, Dr. Peter Corterier, and the Honorable Richard Burt. At the end of the conference, the cochairmen prepared a summary report based on the conference discussions.

This book, which appears after a year of growing public concern for arms control on this side of the Atlantic, contains the conference documents and two additional chapters on negotiating options for INF. Together they provide an excellent analysis of the issues connected with the deployment of nuclear weapons in Europe. These issues are both analytically and politically challenging: intra-alliance relations, public involvement in national-security decisions, nuclear strategy, the meaning of détente.

The authors hold differing viewpoints, and no attempt will be made here to forge a consensus. It does seem to me important, however, that in looking at the fascinating details of the dual decision, its repercussions, and the negotiations in Geneva, we do not neglect the two basic dilemmas that form the backdrop against which the conference in Brussels took place. The first dilemma is inherent in the nature of the alliance. The United States is much stronger militarily than the European allies it is committed to protect. It is separated from them by an ocean. Moreover, the fulfillment of the American commitment to launch nuclear war in Europe's defense could mean the destruction of American as well as European society.

This has led to a basic conflict of interest. The European allies—aware of the destruction any kind of nuclear war would inflict—have tended to favor a deterrent strategy that threatens early all-out nuclear war in response to Soviet aggression. The present U.S. strategy, however, is to put off, until absolutely necessary, escalation to nuclear war. Some (in the United States) have argued that the use of nuclear weapons in Europe might not necessarily lead to a general strategic exchange.

The second dilemma, related to the first, concerns the utility of nuclear weapons. Some argue that nuclear weapons can be used for the pursuit of military objectives, to reverse a disadvantageous battlefield situation arising out of a conventional attack, for example, or during a limited nuclear war to establish escalation dominance that will allow our side to prevail.

Others, among whom I would include myself, believe that nuclear weapons are useful only to deter nuclear war, not to wage war. Moreover, this group believes, as McGeorge Bundy, George Kennan, Robert NcNamara, and I wrote earlier this year, "The one clearly defined firebreak against the worldwide disaster of general nuclear war is the one that stands between all other kinds of conflict and any use whatsoever of nuclear weapons."

The 1979 dual decision is an attempt by NATO to cope with these dilemmas through a military hardware decision. The arguments of the supporters of NATO nuclear modernization illustrate these dilemmas. It is argued that the 572 new missiles are necessary to promote linkage between theater and strategic systems, and that they make deterrence more credible because the United States will not have to threaten suicide to defend Europe. The deployment of missiles is said to meet a real military need, yet the numbers chosen and their basing mode were determined largely by political criteria. The missile deployment is said to be necessary to reassure the alliance, yet the deployment decision may lead to a crisis in Atlantic relations.

Whatever the final outcome of the dual decision and the negotiations in Geneva, NATO's twin dilemmas can no longer be avoided or solved with hardware. They must be addressed directly. In my view, the way to proceed is by a careful reexamination of NATO's reliance on the threat of starting a nuclear war. That, I hope, would lead to a decision to build up conventional forces, so that the alliance need no longer depend on such a threat.

Such a change would have a number of real benefits for the alliance. It would go a long way toward meeting the understandable anxiety that underlies the growing arms control movement here and in Europe. It would make easier the management of nuclear-deterrent forces of both the United States and NATO. In particular, it would no longer be necessary for the United States or NATO to attain capabilities to fight and win a nuclear war at any time. There would be less need to rely on battlefield nuclear weapons. Such a change would also focus NATO attention on the need to improve conventional capabilities in Europe, raising the threshold of nuclear war. Finally, and most importantly, moving toward no first use should in time strengthen the political cohesion of

NATO by creating a military policy the people and governments of the alliance can believe in.

While I believe the policy change I have outlined will help resolve NATO's dilemmas, I am sure the issues surrounding nuclear weapons in Europe will remain difficult and complex. The chapters in this book help clarify these issues and make an important contribution to a debate vital to the security of all the NATO nations.

Gerard C. Smith

Acknowledgments

Shortly after NATO made its 1979 dual decision for nuclear-weapons modernization and limitation, the NATO Information Directorate proposed that the Arms Control Association (ACA) convene a conference in Brussels to air the complex issues raised by the decision. The association's executive director, William H. Kincade, launched the project in 1980 with the assistance of ACA's president, Herbert Scoville, Jr.; vice-president, Barry Carter; and then-treasurer, John Rhinelander. At the NATO Information Directorate, Julia Moore and her successor, Nyoka White, facilitated the task of bringing a Washington-planned conference to Brussels and NATO headquarters.

By September 1981, generous contributions from the W. Averell Harriman Foundation, the Arthur Ross Foundation, the Ford Foundation, The Dreyfus Fund, the Fritz Thyssen Stiftung, and the NATO Information Directorate made possible a rich and lively three-day session.

When planning for the Brussels conference began, the tremendous European public interest in arms control contrasted sharply with public apathy in the United States. Concern now exists on both sides of the Atlantic. We believe the publication of this book, which addresses the central issues of public concern, is well timed to constructively channel this debate.

We are grateful to all the contributors for updating their chapters to make possible the most current account of the issues. Gregory Treverton's and Jane M.O. Sharp's kind permission for us to include their articles strengthens the original contributions by detailing possible negotiating options. Sharp's chapter first appeared in the March 1982 edition of *Arms Control Today*. Treverton's was originally prepared for the ACA Board of Directors.

We are indebted to Robert Scott, who prepared the bibliography, tables, and illustrations; and to Gil Klinger, who developed the glossary and assisted with the graphics. Thanks are also due to Julie Reimer, who typed the manuscript. Finally, this book would not have been possible without the enthusiasm and superb administrative support of Karen Griffin Roberts throughout the conference planning and execution.

The Arms Control Association is a nonpartisan, national-membership organization dedicated to promoting public understanding of effective policies and programs in arms control and disarmament. The views expressed in this book are those of the chapter authors, and do not represent those of the Association or the conference sponsors.

Introduction

At a December 12, 1979, meeting in Brussels, the North Atlantic Treaty Organization (NATO) announced its intent to modernize its nuclear arsenal by deploying a total of 572 new ground-launched long-range missiles. Four-hundred sixty-four are to be deployed as ground-launched cruise missiles (GLCMs) in Great Britain, Italy, The Netherlands, Belgium, and West Germany. The remaining 108 are Pershing II ballistic missiles for deployment in West Germany. These systems would permit NATO to strike Soviet territory from Western Europe missile sites for the first time since the early 1960s. NATO emphasized the decision was not intended to escalate the East-West arms competition, but to close a gap caused by Soviet intermediate-nuclear-force (INF) modernization. To underscore this point, the alliance made a parallel declaration that it was willing to undertake arms control negotiations to stabilize the theater-nuclear balance. Almost two years later, on November 18, 1981, negotiations between the United States and the USSR began in Geneva on the limitation of intermediate-nuclear forces.

The dual decision was an attempt by NATO to deal with three related issues—NATO nuclear doctrine, the changing European nuclear balance, and alliance political factors. Ironically, these same issues now place the NATO decision in jeopardy.

NATO Nuclear Doctrine

All nuclear doctrine is speculative because nuclear war remains an unknown. As a result, a number of unresolved basic questions underlie the military rationale for the use of nuclear weapons in Europe.

First, do nuclear weapons have characteristics that make them uniquely suited for certain kinds of warfare, or could other means better achieve military objectives? For example, some critics of battlefield nuclear weapons argue that any target small enough to move (tanks, aircraft, and so forth) is small enough to be hit with a conventional weapon. Moreover, unlike nuclear weapons, conventional forces can be used at the discretion of the commander, can be moved easily, and do not require political consultation before use. Battlefield nuclear weapons also pose problems to the defense, especially when radiation is carried by shifting winds. Longer-range nuclear weapons have less danger for the defense, but carry greater risk of escalation to intercontinental nuclear exchanges.

Second, no one knows how much destruction from nuclear weapons would be tolerable to one side in its desire to exact a victory in battle; no one knows how much destruction must be threatened to deter adventurism.

Introduction

During the Eisenhower years, these questions were swept aside under *massive retaliation*, a doctrine that required a swift, all-out nuclear response by NATO to any level of aggression by the Warsaw Pact. But as the Soviets developed powerful intermediate- and strategic-nuclear forces in the early 1960s, the doctrine began to lack credibility.

The most important attempt to make doctrine more credible came in 1967, when NATO adopted *flexible response*. As described by Richard Burt, "flexible response . . . commits the alliance to escalate a conflict as high as is needed to defeat any aggression, but permits it to confine a conflict to as low a level as possible consistent with that objective." It was intended to make NATO nuclear policy more credible because the level of NATO response would correspond to the degree of Warsaw Pact attack.

In fact, this doctrine, officially called MC–14/3, is a compromise between European and American interpretations of the appropriate level of response. It reflects, on one hand, the European distaste for either a prolonged conventional war or a nuclear war fought on their territory and, on the other, the American unease with rapid escalation to intercontinental nuclear exchanges with the USSR.

To the Europeans, therefore, the threat of rapid escalation to the intercontinental level is more appropriate to strengthen deterrence and perhaps to spare their territory. To Americans, a longer conventional battle with limited use of tactical and theater nuclear forces is more appropriate. Flexible response—as high as needed and as low as possible—is less a coherent war plan than a classic political compromise: Europeans accept the requirement for initial conventional defense, while the United States reaffirms its readiness to escalate to strategic nuclear war if necessary.

The role of intermediate-nuclear weapons remains unresolved in this basic defense strategy. Ostensibly, INF represents the link between automatic escalation (coupling) to the strategic level, and containment of nuclear exchanges to the theater. As such, they provide an intermediate step between the lowest and highest levels of potential NATO defense. Yet this simple formula merely begs the basic questions: How soon and how much INF are needed to deter Soviet attack, or to wrest a negotiated settlement during the conflict? And, will such use prompt or preclude escalation to the strategic level?

The Alliance lived with this ambiguity in nuclear doctrine until the 1979 two-track decision forced NATO to justify INF deployment on military grounds and to set objectives for INF negotiations. The basic questions came once more to the fore.

Richard Burt summarizes the official doctrinal justification for INF:

> [T]he emplacement of long-range U.S. cruise and ballistic missiles in Europe makes escalation of any nuclear war in Europe more likely, not less. This is why our Allies asked for such a deployment. This is why the United States accepted. This is why the deployment strengthens deterrence.

Klaas de Vries offers a contrasting, European perspective that challenges the foundations of the doctrine itself:

> NATO's strategy of deterrence through flexible response and its reliance on nuclear weapons based in Europe is now seriously at issue. ... While the experts worry that the United States would not use their nuclear systems to defend Europe, public concern is precisely that they will. ... For Europeans—given the destructiveness of nuclear weapons—flexible response in many respects is massive retaliation in another guise.

This dispute over NATO nuclear doctrine hangs over the negotiations and the planned deployments. If left unresolved, it may undermine both.

The Changing European Nuclear Balance

In 1954, the NATO Council decided to introduce battlefield (or tactical) nuclear weapons into Europe. Their purpose was to compensate for Soviet conventional superiority and to signal the intent to use nuclear weapons early on in any conflict (although specific-employment strategy remained vague). Between 1959 and 1963, intermediate-range ballistic missiles (IRBMs) were deployed in response to Soviet missiles then being pointed at Western Europe.

These Thor and Jupiter missiles, according to Gregory Treverton, "were viewed from the start by the United States as a stopgap: once intercontinental ballistic missiles in the United States could cover all the Soviet targets of interest, the need for the IRBMs would fade. With the rapid build-up of American ICBMs in the early 1960s, the IRBMs were withdrawn by 1964." Upon withdrawal, sixty-two Polaris sea-based missiles were assigned to NATO.

As Jane Sharp points out:

> By the late 1970s, NATO's nuclear arsenal comprised a modest British force of Polaris SLBMs, medium-range Vulcan bombers, and shorter-range Buccaneer strike aircraft—fully integrated into NATO strike plans—plus an American NATO-assigned force of several hundred Polaris SLBMs and carrier-based aircraft, and somewhere between 7,000 and 10,000 warheads for use on land-based systems, demolition mines, and a variety of short-range missiles and artillery pieces.

In contrast to American deployments, which emphasize battlefield systems, Soviet deployments reflect a view of Europe as a strategic target. Sharp notes that, until recently, "the Soviet Union has placed less emphasis on short-range battlefield weapons and long-range manned bombers." They have, instead, given greater emphasis to INF missiles. Moreover, as Treverton points out, "early Soviet INF deployments of SS–4s and SS–5s in the late fifties kept Europe 'hostage' against American nuclear superiority." This

Introduction

American superiority at the strategic level, according to Richard Burt, "provided the margin of security that permitted shortfalls in other areas of NATO's force structure." As a result, NATO did not seem to notice the Soviet preponderance in land-based INF. Indeed, the 1960s withdrawal of Thors and Jupiters reinforced this asymmetry.

By the late 1970s, however, events changed the outlook of key NATO officials. The Soviet Union had begun to dismantle the SS–4s and SS–5s, replace them with the more accurate SS–20, and deploy the new Backfire bomber. This modernization effort was widely interpreted as a qualitative leap in Soviet capabilities, which, in combination with a Soviet conventional build-up, made the theater balance swing uncomfortably to Warsaw Pact advantage. At the same time, the United States lost its nuclear superiority as the Soviet Union achieved nuclear parity, codified by ongoing negotiations in SALT II. This, according to some observers, accentuated the disparities at lower levels of nuclear forces, and made the Soviet modernization appear more formidable. Finally, the American nuclear guarantee, as the ultimate deterrent, appeared less than absolute when concern increased that U.S. land-based missiles were vulnerable to a Soviet first strike.

Many of these arguments were brought to public attention by Schmidt's 1977 Alastair Buchan Memorial Lecture before the International Institute for Strategic Studies (IISS). His views are echoed by Peter Corterier, who points to the widening Soviet superiority in INF in the midst of a SALT-accepted intercontinental parity: "Thus, the prime purpose of the demand for modernization of the Alliance's INF capability, as contained in the two-track decision, is to reduce the disparity that has emerged."

While many in NATO countries share Schmidt's and Corterier's views on the changing European nuclear balance, there is intense public debate on the subject. As Andrew Pierre points out, the facts of the Soviet military build-up, including an almost threefold increase in SS–20 deployments since 1979, are not at issue; the consequences of that build-up are. Many analysts, arguing from a different interpretation of deterrence, believe the recent numerical changes are not significant. Given a rough parity between U.S. and Soviet nuclear forces worldwide, individual-theater balances are not very important. What is important is a strong U.S. commitment to defend Europe. The easiest way to break that commitment, it is argued, is to deploy new INF in Europe. The battle would then be limited to Europe, letting American territory go free.

The 1979 NATO decision is consistent with the Schmidt view of recent changes in the European nuclear balance. However, military factors alone did not drive the decision.

Alliance Political Factors

Andrew Pierre highlights "the ambiguity and inconclusiveness of the military arguments for and against NATO's INF modernization program" and concludes that "with the doctrinal issues remaining unclear and not providing a sound base for justifying the decisions of government, it is the political factors that have become paramount."

To Pierre, politics has always been at the root of key alliance decisions about the deployment of long-range nuclear weapons. This was true in the 1950s with Thors and Jupiters, in the 1960s with the Multilateral Force (MLF), and in the 1970s with cruise and Pershing II missiles. Josef Joffe makes a similar point by comparing the latter two decisions. He concludes that the 1979 NATO deployment decision is "a cleverly balanced political compromise whose strategic objective, like that of the MLF, remains in the dark."

The two cases, says Joffe, provide "an instructive case study in irony: solutions dramatized dilemmas; unifying moves deepened dissension; American accomodation to presumed European wishes spawned resentment and hostility among America's allies." A review of political issues leading up to and following the 1979 decision illustrates these ironies.

In 1977 and 1978, European leaders became concerned that the United States, in its eagerness to reach agreement with the Soviets on SALT, was neglecting the security interests of Western Europe. The perceived weakness of the Carter administration accentuated existing fears of growing East-West gap in military hardware, caused largely by Soviet SS–20 deployments. The cruise missile became a handle for European pressure for reassurance. As Joffe notes, "For the Germans, cruise missiles assumed . . . a symbolic quality —as a measure of the American commitment to German security and German interests."

By 1979, NATO leaders felt something had to be done. The result was the dual decision.

To display the American resolve convincingly, the NATO experts felt that new nuclear links in the deterrence chain had to be visible, and thus ground based. Because of traditional European apprehensiveness about a nuclear-armed Germany, the West German government established the nonsingularity principle, requiring at least one other continental NATO power to deploy the cruise missiles. In addition, the United States had to assume control over the nuclear forces.

At the same time, however, NATO leaders realized that modernization might not succeed without a parallel arms control track. The West Germans in particular had long followed a dual policy of defense and détente toward the East. Indeed, Schmidt's 1977 IISS speech expressing concern about the balance was equally vociferous on the need for U.S.–Soviet negotiations on INF in the context of what was then called SALT III. Peter Corterier summarizes the German view: "To us, defense efforts and arms control are equal, necessary, and complementary components of a realistic security policy."

Introduction   xvii

Moreover, NATO as an organization established the two-pronged approach in 1967, when the Harmel Report emphasized that defense preparedness and détente with the East should guide NATO's policy.

Finally, the neutron-bomb incident in 1977–1978 gave a clear indication of how strong the public aversion to new nuclear deployments was likely to be. Accordingly, the arms control element was considered essential in order to garner the necessary parliamentary and public support for modernization.

However, the 1979 solution only dramatized NATO's dilemmas. The visibility of the new Pershings and GLCMs—deemed necessary for strengthening U.S.-European political ties—prompted adverse public reaction that grew steadily stronger through 1980 and 1981.

In October 1981, approximately 250,000 people demonstrated against nuclear weapons in Bonn, London, and Rome. In November 1981, 400,000 marched in Amsterdam. In West Germany, over two million have signed the Krefeld Appeal to stop new INF deployments.

There is serious doubt the Dutch will ever accept missiles on their soil, and the Belgians have strong reservations. In Britain, the opposition Labour Party has come out against the missiles, and, in West Germany, the Social Democratic Party SPD is split over the issue. Though there is broad popularity in Europe for the antinuclear movement, it is not anti-American or antidefense. Support for NATO still remains strong in all major West European countries, although an increase in neutralism has also been registered. Despite the trends, which cannot be discounted, in 1981 over 60 percent of Britons and West Germans favored the deployment of new missiles as long as they are linked to negotiations.

There are a number of reasons for this politically powerful opposition to the NATO decision to modernize nuclear weapons. First, a general divergence in U.S. and European attitudes on détente began to appear in the late 1970s. As described by Peter Corterier, the Americans saw détente as bringing benefits only to the Soviets, while Europeans saw improvements in human contacts and economic relations with the East. When the superpower conflict heats up, Germans fear "losing the precious security gains and improved human contacts." By 1981, the Reagan administration was flexing new-found American muscle and Europeans seemed in search of the status quo ante Afghanistan. In this setting, Joffe notes, "it is hard to recall a previous period in the history of the Alliance when our moods were as incongruent as they are today."

To Joffe, Pierre, and de Vries, arms control brings these contrasting views into sharp relief. To Europeans, arms control symbolizes détente. The SALT process was at the center of the decade of détente, with the SALT II Treaty its hallmark. Even the 1979 Brussels decision assumed the political and military conditions of SALT II ratification.

But the Reagan administration campaigned on the claim that SALT II was fatally flawed. This polarized even further the attitudes toward arms control policy on either side of the Atlantic. As Joffe describes the disparity, "Europeans are prone to regard armament efforts as provocation and arms control as an end in itself; Americans tend to view arms control as a past gateway for Soviet opportunism, and rearmament as a prime guarantee for future Soviet restraint."

Klaas de Vries sees "the American shift on arms control" as causing much of the public unrest in Europe over nuclear weapons. With a two-year gap between the 1979 decision and the beginning of talks aimed at limiting INF, the public mind dwelled only on deployments and the consequences of being a target in nuclear war. Loose talk from Reagan administration officials about the possibility of fighting limited nuclear war in Europe fed fears that were incited earlier by Carter administration policy on the neutron bomb and P.D.-59. As a result, the debate finally focused on the most fundamental issue: the NATO nuclear doctrine of flexible response.

As de Vries put it, "Public opinion is now alive to the contradictions in NATO's present strategy." The cochairmen's report from the Arms Control Association's Brussels conference summarizes the significance of this new public-opinion factor:

> NATO should take account of the commonsense view—underlying much of the public apprehension—that weapons designed to discourage aggression by influencing adversary perceptions always risk affecting these perceptions in a provocative, rather than a sobering way. This recognition, as much as any other, accounts for the shift in public attitudes since 1979. . . . A failure to address public concerns adequately could seriously impair the ability of the Western nations to implement their decisions as an Alliance.

Arms Control and the Future of the Alliance

The arms control track of the 1979 NATO decision is heavily burdened by an array of technical and political issues. On the technical side, as Treverton explains, "the overriding puzzle in the Geneva negotiations is how they could be used to create a balance where none now exists. . . . Different constructions of the INF balance . . . obviously affect the result, but no reasonable construction comes close to eliminating the puzzle." This situation is exacerbated by the two-track decision. As de Vries points out, "in the modernization program, NATO stressed that it did not aim for numerical parity (just a matching capability), whereas in the arms control package, the Alliance has insisted that the right to numerical parity must be established."

Given this basic problem of evaluating the balance, it is not surprising that President Reagan, and Chairman Brezhnev's opening bids for the Geneva talks were far apart. Reagan's zero option, announced in November 1981, calls for the elimination of all Soviet land-based intermediate missiles in exchange for no new NATO deployments of cruise and Pershing II missiles.

Chairman Brezhnev countered by proposing one-third reductions in all NATO and Warsaw Pact delivery vehicles—with a freedom to mix on land, sea, and air—phased in by 1990. He had earlier proposed a moratorium on all new deployments during the course of negotiations.

The two sides clearly disagree on numbers. By Brezhnev's count, the sides are fairly equal; to Reagan, the United States trails by a factor of six. But even if the sides did agree on numbers, several technical questions will complicate the process of classifying and trading off systems, as the following examples show.

Differences in Force Composition, Capability, and Mission

Most of the Soviet forces are long-range theater systems. Most of NATO's forces are shorter-range or battlefield nuclear weapons. Moreover, the core of the Soviet long-range INF systems consists of land-based missiles. NATO's long-range systems are mainly aircraft and include, as of 1982, no missiles. A further complication is that NATO's inventory of long-range systems includes some U.S. strategic forces (Poseidon SLBMs) allocated to the Supreme Allied Commander Europe (SACEUR).

Duality of Mission and Capability

Both aircraft and missiles have variable ranges and many may carry either nuclear or conventional ordnance, permitting them to be used for tactical, theater, or strategic missions. These systems cut across the distinctions that have long been important to U.S. and NATO nuclear-weapons doctrine. They have been labeled gray-area systems. Their ambiguities pose problems both for negotiating forces levels and for verification of these levels. Cruise missiles present special difficulties because they are small, easily concealed, can carry either conventional or nuclear warheads, and may vary in range or be launched from a variety of platforms.

Differences in Geography

The USSR faces intermediate-range forces from China, France, and Great Britain, in addition to the United States. This raises the problem of compensating for weapons from countries that are not officially participants in the bilateral talks.

Though these technical issues will have a serious impact on the negotiations, the critical questions affecting a positive outcome are political. First, can the East-West relationship, now fragile, remain insulated from competitive pressures until an agreement can be crafted? Second, will the Alliance decision remain intact and not succumb to either Soviet or internal pressures? Finally, will public opinion in individual NATO countries permit the deployment of new missiles through 1988 if an agreement falls short of President Reagan's zero option?

With these factors in mind, both Jane M.O. Sharp and Gregory Treverton review the possible negotiating approaches and conclude that a quick and limited agreement is best, though not without problems. This would take the form of "an early agreement to codify mutually agreeable aspects of the status quo," according to Sharp. At some point, of course, it would still be necessary to address the other rungs of the nuclear ladder—short-range and strategic systems. START negotiations will initially cover the latter, but could, over time, incorporate INF. If reductions cannot be achieved in INF in the status quo approach, they could be accomplished later.

The critical requirement is to hold the Alliance together in the process. Different observers have different prescriptions. Some, including de Vries, contend that the original rationale for the 1979 decision (that is, the modernization) must be reviewed if the arms control talks are to succeed and NATO is to stay united. Others, including Pierre, believe that Alliance cohesion and purpose would be seriously endangered if the 1979 decision unravels, and, to prevent this, progress on arms control is imperative.

NATO has straddled its ambiguities with reasonable success for three decades. It now has to manage the old paradoxes and new ironies under the added complication of a watchful public eye.

1

Nuclear Weapons in Europe: Perspectives in Negotiations

Elliot L. Richardson and
Henri Simonet

Specialists on political and security affairs from nine countries in the North Atlantic Alliance (NATO) met in Brussels from September 21–23, 1981, to review the issues of nuclear weapons in Europe, giving special attention to the question of limitation or reduction of such weapons. Four papers on these issues were prepared for the conference. Prior to the working sessions, the twenty-four participants were briefed by officials of NATO and SHAPE. At plenary sessions during the conference, the participants heard addresses by Staats Minister, Herr Doctor Peter Corterier of the Federal Republic of Germany, and by the Honorable Richard Burt, director of the Bureau of Politico-Military Affairs of the U.S. Department of State. The conference was sponsored by the Arms Control Association, a private U.S. organization, with the assistance of the NATO Information Directorate, the Royal Institute for International Relations (Brussels), and private West European and North American foundations.

The conference participants—none of whom was serving in the government of his country at the time of the conference—were united in their concern for the future security and well-being of the peoples of Western Europe and North America. Yet, they reflected a variety of viewpoints on the most desirable means of achieving those goals. The areas of agreement and disagreement are here summarized as a way of establishing a framework for joint action and an agenda of problems requiring future resolution, in the hope of assisting the work of alliance governments on a matter of common and paramount concern.

Background

The issues addressed by the participants have several, related sources. Most prominent among them are (1) the codification of parity in intercontinental nuclear weapons between the United States and the USSR by the signing of the

This chapter was prepared by the conference cochairmen and reflects their views. It does not seek to portray all of the substance of the discussions or the views of each of the twenty-five participants.

SALT II agreements (currently being observed by both nations, though ratified by neither), (2) the ongoing deployment by the Soviet Union of new and more capable intermediate- or theater-range nuclear weapons (SS–20 missile and Backfire bomber), and (3) the 1979 decision by the members of NATO to deploy 464 ground-launched cruise missiles (GLCMs) and 108 advanced Pershing II ballistic missiles and, at the same time, to seek limits or reductions for these long-range theater nuclear forces (LRTNF) through East-West negotiations.

The conference reviewed the evolution of nuclear forces and doctrine in NATO and the Warsaw Pact Organization (WPO), assessed the impact of Soviet and NATO LRTNF deployment on the overall military balance, examined the differences among the Atlantic Alliance members with regard to political and security objectives or approaches, evaluated the climate and influence of public opinion in the NATO countries, looked at the implementation by NATO of its 1979 dual decision, and studied various options for achieving negotiated limits or reductions.

Conference discussions reflected a considerable diversity of viewpoint, which is both a problem for and the strength of democratic societies. Where one stands on the complex LRTNF issue depends on which of the many elements of the matter seem most important to the individual. The different positions seen in the NATO countries can be typified by how they stress the three recurring, but sometimes conflicting, elements of NATO policy—detente, deterrence, and defense—and by how they believe these goals can be harmonized and achieved. In examining the question of nuclear weapons in Europe, the conference sought to look at each of the many factors in terms of their effect on these three objectives.

The Military Dimensions of LRTNF

Any review of the issue of nuclear weapons in Europe must begin with an assessment of the European military balance. At briefings from NATO officials, including Secretary-General Luns, and at the conferees' first session, the participants were given the chance to assess critically the military situation facing NATO. On the basis of these briefings and discussions, the cochairmen believe the military balance—while by no means as desperately unfavorable to the West as some alarmists have claimed—contains elements of concern. We share the judgment of Ivan Selin (chapter 2) that

> the forces arrayed in or available to both sides in Germany are very large and very strong, though the relative advantage must go to the Pact. The Pact could not count on a quick breakthrough and would be likely to find a nonnuclear war lasting a long time and, therefore, bearing great risk of escalation to one of the higher levels of violence involving nuclear weapons. Nevertheless, the West must conclude that its forces do not promise success in a nonnuclear war; NATO counts on risk, political considerations, and nuclear weapons to deter nonnuclear war in Central Europe.

We believe an important conclusion flows from this evaluation. Some of the conferees argued that NATO's conventional forces should be strengthened to deter a conventional Soviet attack and lessen the pressures for first use of nuclear weapons by the NATO alliance. The cochairmen believe this argument has a great deal of validity. We are aware, of course, that NATO has historically resisted pressure to improve conventional defenses, partly for economic reasons. We believe, however, that the use of new conventional-weapons technologies and tactics emphasizing speed and mobility can improve conventional-force capabilities without a major increase in expenditures.

Turning more directly to the role of nuclear weapons in Europe, the conference discussions emphasized that the doctrine under which NATO plans to use nuclear weapons—flexible response—embraces several perspectives on the use of nuclear weapons. Critics believe that, since it is a compromise, NATO's nuclear doctrine is insufficient. The cochairmen do not share this view. While not ruling out further refinement of flexible response, the cochairmen believe it is sufficient for NATO's needs. The key to deterrence is to ensure that no potential aggressor could be certain he could avoid catastrophic damage in a massive attack on Europe. NATO's doctrine of flexible response insures that massive Soviet attack carries a high risk of escalation, inflicting unacceptable damage on the aggressor.

After looking at the military balance in Europe and NATO doctrine, the conference focused on the origins of the dual decision to modernize NATO's TNF and proceed toward arms control negotiations. In particular, the conferees were concerned with laying out the original rationale for the dual decision and asking whether it still made political and military sense. On the first topic, there was general agreement that the NATO decision was made for a combination of political and military reasons. Militarily, the United States and its NATO partners had concluded, by the middle and late 1970s, that some of their aging LRTNF systems—especially Pershing I and the long-range Vulcan and F-111 bombers—had to be modernized. Moreover, many NATO officials believed that—with the achievement of strategic parity between the United States and the USSR—disparities in other forces, especially LRTNF, acquired relatively greater significance. This was the thrust of Chancellor Schmidt's Alastair Buchan Lecture in 1977. In this context, the continuing Soviet buildup of Backfire bombers and SS–20 missiles assumed special importance. Further, NATO officials felt there should be some symmetry in territorial vulnerability between the Soviet Union and NATO Europe. This did not mean that NATO was to be given the capability to fight a nuclear war independent of the U.S. arsenal. It did mean that NATO should act to lessen the potential danger to the Europeans of Soviet attempts at coercion backed up by the SS–20 and Backfire.

Politically, Alliance officials believed it was important that NATO respond to the Soviet buildup by demonstrating its resolve, emphasizing the shared Alliance responsibilities and reaffirming the U.S. nuclear guarantee.

Figure 1-1. Major Intermediate-Range Nuclear Weapons Deployments in Europe

Perspectives on Negotiations

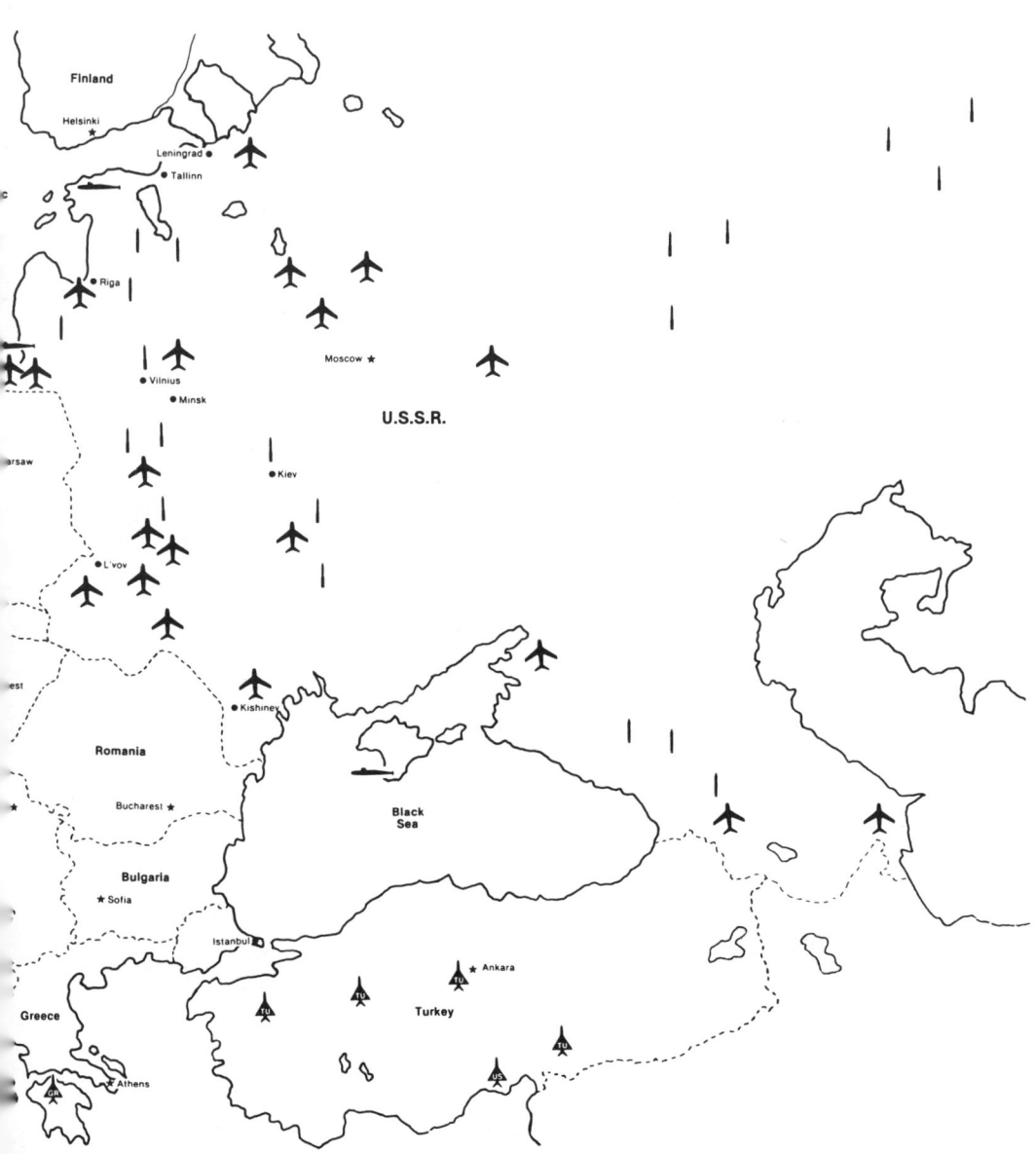

Sources: Arms Race and Nuclear Weapons Research Project, Institute for Policy Studies; U.S. Department of Defense, *Soviet Military Power;* NATO, *NATO and the Warsaw Pact Force Comparisons;* John Collins, *US-Soviet Military Balance;* "Air Force Almanac," *Air Force Magazine,* May 1982; US Air Force, *Soviet Aerospace Handbook;* US Congress. Senate. Committee on Foreign Relations. *United States Foreign Policy Objectives and Overseas Military Installations,* 1979.

Just as important, the Alliance wanted to show it was still concerned with preserving detente and would deal with threats to security through negotiations where possible.

As might be expected, the conferees differed most strongly on whether or not these rationales for the original decision had continuing relevance today. The cochairman believe they do. In particular, we would emphasize that a failure to stand by the dual decision would lead to bitter recrimination on both sides of the Atlantic, thus weakening the NATO Alliance—which remains the most crucial element in Western security. Equally important, we believe—as we stress later in this chapter—standing by the double decision offers the best hope of securing Soviet agreement to limits on their LRTNF, which can further increase Western security.

The Political Dimensions of LRTNF

The differences between NATO partners, within member governments and across the Atlantic on Alliance nuclear policy were evident at the conference. While such diversity and controversy is not new to the Alliance, the current LRTNF debate differs substantially from earlier disagreements because of the far greater interest and attention of publics, now more informed on these questions. The cochairmen shared the hope that pursuit of the arms control portion of the dual decision could go a long way toward resolving some of the differences. Yet we were also aware that this imposes an additional burden on a negotiating process already intrinsically complicated.

The cochairmen are mindful that the rather narrow and technical issues involved in LRTNF are, for the public in many of the NATO countries, potent symbols of much broader and deeper concerns, such as the role of force in international relations, the likelihood and consequences of nuclear war, and the impact of arms procurement on the possibility of conflict. At the same time, the theoretical formulations surrounding the basic concept of deterrence have now become so complex in their implications that publics cannot easily comprehend the operation of deterrence and sometimes resist or reject its consequences. Finally, the very process of arms control has come under a cloud of suspicion, in part because more rapid and deeper reductions in nuclear forces were promised than it has been possible to achieve in practice. As a result of these factors, both aspects of the dual decision of nuclear-weapons modernization and limitation lack credibility with many people.

While specialists and officials have tried to make clear the justification for LRTNF, to restore the reputation of arms control and to detach these questions from the larger concerns animating public opinion, these efforts have thus far met with only limited success. Though it may be true that what has been termed the democratization of nuclear decision making in the West complicates the issues within governments and within and between alliances, the cochairmen believe that, in democracies, this process of growing public participation in nuclear policy is inevitable and legitimate, to the extent that it involves civil and informed debate. We consider, further, that NATO should redouble its efforts to satisfy the public's concerns, in particular by moving with all deliberate speed to the negotiating table with reasonable proposals. In addition, NATO should, recognizing the need for confidentiality in preparations and negotiations, give as much visibility as possible to its arms-limitations efforts, as well as to its modernization program. The biannual review of the dual decision provides one opportunity for exposing the issue, and the meetings of the Special Consultative Group provide another. NATO should take account of the commonsense view—underlying much of the public apprehension—that weapons designed to discourage aggression by influencing adversary perceptions always risk affecting these perceptions in a provocative, rather than a sobering way. This recognition, as much as any other, accounts for the shift in public attitudes since 1979, and, as publics critical of alliance policy seem to be aware, merely restating NATO's pacific intentions to deter war with improved weapons may not fully limit the risks of unintended consequences. A failure to address public concerns adequately could seriously impair the ability of the Western nations to implement their decision as an alliance.

The cochairmen also feel, however, that the influence the LRTNF modernization may have on these risks should not be exaggerated. There are already many nuclear weapons in both East and West Europe that have awesome destructive power, yet could act as magnets for opposing weapons in the event of a conflict. The dual decision unequivocally provided for a reduction of 1,000 Western warheads—irrespective of negotiations—almost double the number that would be introduced by NATO LRTNF modernization, if completed. These 1,000 warheads have since been removed. If both halves of the NATO decision are not implemented, Western Europe may forfeit the opportunity to begin a process that will lead to even more substantial cuts in nuclear-weapons levels.

In terms of the political climate of the alliance, the cochairmen, while recognizing the desirability of reviewing the status and implications of the strategic-arms-limitation process, are struck by the negative impact that uncertainty about the continuation of this process has on West European opinion. Though all of the NATO members have taken significant steps to make clear their interest in getting on with LRTNF negotiations, there will always be some doubt about the pace and genuineness of arms control in European political circles, so long as the fate of the limits on intercontinental nuclear weapons remains ambiguous.

Approaches to Negotiating NATO Security

The cochairmen approach the arms control component of the dual decision with several strongly held convictions. First, the goal of arms limitation is to enhance the security of the peoples of Western Europe. Second, any arms control agreements must be politically viable, that is, there must be a reasonable expectation that they will command the support of publics in the NATO countries. To meet these criteria, agreements must (and must be seen to) make a substantial start in slowing and, in time, halting the nuclear-arms competition reflected in the alternating modernization cycles of the two alliance systems. Finally, and most importantly, arms reduction must lessen the likelihood of nuclear war in Europe and elsewhere.

While our review of the conditions influencing negotiations revealed many difficult issues, we are satisfied that there are no insuperable obstacles to successful negotiations. A ceiling, in the first instance, on the numbers of long-range theater nuclear weapons in both the East and the West continues to serve the joint interest of lessening the threat of nuclear war while also serving the separate security interests of both sides. We also see opportunities for making the trade-offs among different types of systems that are essential when bargaining over dissimilar forces with varied and differing missions. We saw disagreement over, but no barrier to finding, a counting system that could embrace these differences.

We believe the guidelines contained in the NATO communique of December 1979 regarding verfiability, equality "both in rights and ceilings," and step-by-step negotiations in the context of the strategic-arms–limitation process remain sound and valid.

While there is agreement in Western Europe and North America on most of the principles underlying negotiations, they do not furnish specific answers to the requirements of developing a negotiating strategy or position. We found instructive on this point (presented during a conference discussion) a typology presented at the conference:

> The "Zero-NATO Option" wherein NATO would deploy no new long-range theater nuclear weapons in return for less-than-total cutbacks in the Soviet SS–20 force.
>
> The "Both-Zero Option," often referred to simply as the "Zero Option," which envisages Soviet dismantling of its SS–20 force in exchange for a NATO commitment not to deploy GLCMs or Pershing II missiles.
>
> The "Mixed Option" envisioning partial reductions of both bomber and missile systems, reductions in only certain types of systems, reductions by one side early in return for later reductions by the other side, or similar trade-offs.

While each of these alternatives can, in some sense, be made compatible with the NATO dual decision, each has its obvious difficulties. The cochairmen believe that, initially, some form of mixed approach offers the best chance of achieving the arms control and security goals we are committed to.

In carrying out such an approach, NATO, we believe, should insist on a principle of equality in numbers of both launchers and warheads, taking account of differences in capabilities between, for example, cruise missiles and ballistic missiles. The concept of equality should also include willingness to reach agreement at lower levels, including significant reductions in SS–20 deployment.

In this context, several negotiating objectives came to our attention that we believe merit the attention and study of NATO.

We agree that it would be desirable to frame the talks so that they address first those systems that threaten major military forces on both sides and that are, therefore, the most likely to provoke attack in a crisis. To some degree, this approach is already implied in the focus on long-range theater nuclear forces. We think, too, that the discussions should have as an important objective raising the so-called nuclear threshold to as high a level as possible.

We note that—because of its range and accuracy—the Pershing II missile is perceived by the Soviet Union as a significant threat to its command and control system and, perhaps, to its major military forces, and thus must be a high-priority target for Soviet military planners and possibly an incentive for an even greater buildup in Soviet forces. This perception, we feel, nevertheless provides the West with a strong position for forthcoming concessions from the USSR on their long-range theater nuclear forces that threaten the West.

We take seriously the notion that, at a minimum, discussions must prevent the nuclear situation in Europe from becoming worse. As part of a mixed approach, therefore, we consider it essential that any limitation on the SS–20 missile be framed so as to preclude its replacement by an even more advanced, follow-on ballistic missile that is now believed to be in development.

We recognize that LRTNF and any agreements covering them make little sense if there are no constraints on intercontinental nuclear forces to which they are inextricably linked, both militarily and politically. We firmly believe that the LRTNF discussions are the necessary and appropriate follow-on to the initial SALT limits on offensive intercontinental nuclear weapons, as provided for in the 1979 dual decision. We see the forthcoming talks as carrying forward in logical fashion the work begun in SALT, but we do not see any need to delay LRTNF negotiations or even the conclusion of an agreement while limits on intercontinental systems are under review.

Indeed, we consider it worth examining whether agreements on intercontinental and long-range theater forces should be combined in a single, comprehensive approach. This implies a single global ceiling on all intercontinental and long-range–theater weapons with regional subceilings. Each party would have the freedom to mix under the subceilings, and would thus be constrained to give up some of one type of system for more of another.

Increasing the intercontinental systems would mean decreasing theater systems.

This approach has the advantage of tying the U.S. deterrent more closely to nuclear weapons based in Western Europe. Several variations on this theme could be developed that take advantage of the experience gained in the strategic-arms-limitation process. Moreover, it meets the requirement of the NATO decision that LRTNF negotiations take place in the context of the strategic- or intercontinental-weapons-limitation process.

We agree with the idea that NATO must remain flexible regarding what should be included in or excluded from talks on long-range theater nuclear forces. Yet we also believe that it only makes sense to concentrate in the first instance on the systems that have encouraged the start of negotiations in the first place, namely, the SS–20 ballistic missile, the Backfire bomber, the U.S. ground-launched cruise missile, and the Pershing II ballistic missile. However, focusing on these systems, or on just long-range missiles alone, should not preclude consideration of widening the agenda so as to be able to negotiate offsetting packages of unlike systems, as was done so successfully with the intercontinental systems (where MIRVed ICBMs and cruise-missile bombers are counted under the same ceiling).

We also think that the time remaining before the first deployment of modern Western LRTNF in 1983 offers an especially good opportunity for negotiating agreements that will permit a balance of LRTNF at the lowest possible level. We urge that maximum advantage be taken of this opportunity. We recognize that negotiations would be greatly facilitated—and that further aggravation of the nuclear competition could be avoided—by a proposal made by several participants for a moratorium only on the further deployment of LRTNF while talks are in progress.

Having been informed of the NATO deliberations on the Alliance position for the discussions (which will be conducted bilaterally between the United States and USSR), we are heartened by the progress that has been made so far in NATO's Special Consultative Group in developing a unified position. However, we feel that no opportunity should be missed for informing publics as much as possible of the concrete steps that NATO is taking through the Special Consultative Group to implement the arms control portion of the dual decision. We are also encouraged to learn that the dual decision is regularly reviewed on a biannual basis and consider that this reassessment should be taken seriously, so as to permit alterations that may be necessitated by changing technical or political circumstances.

While we believe there is sound reason to hold out considerable hope for an arms-reduction achievement in the forthcoming talks, we believe it is important to recall that, with only a few exceptions, arms control to date has succeeded primarily in preventing the deployment of new weapons, not in reducing the numbers of existing ones. We think it would be a serious mistake to hope that these talks would clear up all concerns and reach zero levels of forces in the first agreement. Arms control, it cannot be emphasized strongly enough, is a process and one that requires small steps before bigger ones can be made. Halting and then reversing the nuclear spiral will require that it first be slowed down. Too great an expectation of complete and final success at the first step can be as harmful to this process as an expectation of failure. Nevertheless, we believe that the issues involved require of both sides that they make progress more rapidly than they have in strategic-arms limitation and in mutual- and balanced-force reductions.

The cochairmen consider that a variety of foreseeable but different outcomes from arms control talks would be consistent with NATO military objectives and nuclear-weapons doctrine, depending on how the particular limits or reductions affect Soviet nuclear forces. Further reductions beyond the 1,000 warheads already removed require consultation and negotiation, which is possible only through the politico-military apparatus provided by the Alliance. We believe, therefore, that NATO plays a vital role in achieving, first, ceilings on and then reductions in theater nuclear forces and in lessening the threat they pose to Western safety. Indeed, we could imagine no realistic scenario wherein the number of nuclear weapons in Europe would be less if NATO were disregarded or bypassed.

The ultimate level of NATO deployment of LRTNF is, in our view, highly sensitive to the actions of the Soviet Union before and during the forthcoming negotiations. We trust that no conditions will be attached to the discussions that would impede their initiation or progress, and that no credit be given to the idea that the prospective Western deployment could be forestalled by avoiding negotiations. Although both East and West may make some unilateral changes in their force levels and dispositions, the best hope for significant reductions and for ending the modernization spiral lies in successful and ongoing negotiations. Such negotiations can only proceed in an atmosphere of good faith on both sides.

If both parties continue to see, as they apparently now do, that their separate and mutual interests in security and the avoidance of nuclear war are best served by negotiating reductions in these terrible engines of war, then we are convinced that arms control can help to meet NATO's objectives of defense, deterrence, and detente. In the absence of a continuing perception of separate but similar interests, we fear the consequences of an aggravated competition in ever more capable theater-nuclear weapons. Yet, while arms reduction has historically begun with painfully small steps, we believe it is possible to look forward to the time when realistically motivated and conducted negotiations—serving as confidence-building measures within and between alliances—will lead to significantly decreased-dependence on nuclear weapons in both East and West. The sooner both sides proceed with this process, the better chance there will be of achieving lower levels.

2 Military Factors in Europe

Ivan Selin

Arms control in Europe can be discussed sensibly only after discussing levels and trends in military forces. The military strategy of Western Europe is to deter attacks by the forces of the Warsaw Pact at any level of violence, while making resort to the next level of violence even more unattractive to the Pact. The theory behind this strategy is that commanders of Warsaw Pact forces should believe, at each level of violence, that (1) an attack is not likely to succeed; (2) if it does not succeed, resort to a higher level of violence is even less likely to succeed; and (3) in the unlikely event that an attack were succeeding, the West itself could threaten credibly to go to the next level of violence and thus put the forces of the Pact at risk. Although the strategy of the West is clothed in the language of deterrence, note that this strategy requires a credible threat on the part of the West to escalate. Thus, the idea that one side will necessarily limit itself to the defensive does not hold up. Each side can threaten to initiate each level of violence, and, in fact, both sides practice both offense and defense.

These simple sentences hide a great deal of ambiguity:

What are the different levels of violence?

What constitutes a successful defense against each level of attack?

What constitutes unacceptable risk to Pact forces?

And of course, does the Warsaw Pact have a strategy that is sufficiently close to that of the West for these distinctions to make any difference?

These are questions that military strategists will argue at great length, coming up with a variety of answers. However the one indisputable fact underlying all the debate is that the strategic forces of the United States are less credible, as a deterrent to less-than-strategic nuclear attacks, than they were in the late 1960s and early 1970s. As the realization grows of the limitations to the use of U.S. strategic forces to deter lower levels of violence, military attention in Europe turns to conventional and tactical nuclear forces.

Levels of Violence

Political scientists can define and discuss in infinitesimal gradation the levels of violence, but for planners of European forces they come down to five, with one troublesome half-level.

The lowest level is a nonnuclear attack—limited in geography. NATO has long debated whether it is necessary to be able to meet a Soviet thrust in Norway or Turkey at the point of attack, or if it would suffice to rely on political arguments and the threat to counterattack elsewhere.

The next level is large-scale conventional attack across the Central European front. The issue here is the duration of conventional war for which it is necessary to prepare: should the target be able to sustain defense and counterattacks for, say, thirty days, or is it necessary to provide for an indefinite, World War II–type war?

The third level is a massive conventional attack coupled with battlefield-nuclear weapons, tactical missiles, artillery, and air-to-ground weapons. The troublesome half-level is conventional attack coupled with chemical, but not nuclear, weapons. The Soviets have such an overwhelming advantage in chemical weapons and defenses that the West is forced to rely on the threat of tactical nuclear weapons to deter this half-level of attack.

The fourth level of attack involves long-range-theater nuclear forces—or Eurostrategic forces—that is, long-range Soviet-based nuclear forces targeted on Western Europe and similar European-based forces targeted on the USSR.

The fifth level involves United States- and Soviet-based strategic forces targeted against each other's country.

The Conventional Balance in Central Europe

The role of nuclear weapons in Western Europe is primarily one of deterrence—not only to deter the Soviet use of nuclear weapons, but also to deter their use of conventional and chemical weapons at the next-lower level of violence. Now that the West has lost its clear superiority in nuclear-armed forces at all levels, its first use of nuclear weapons has lost whatever credibility it might once have had to deter Pact actions below the level of massive attack. However, nuclear weapons are, in fact, the ultimate guarantor of safety from conventional war, especially war of the drawn-out type that the two world wars became. Thus if we are interested in the military factors governing nuclear weapons in Europe, we must start with the conventional balance.

The first level of conflict—limited-conventional warfare—could not conceivably be countered by nuclear weapons. The West has no alternative but to hope that the political costs and the (faint) threat of NATO military intrusion elsewhere would continue to deter a Soviet grab of Finnmark, Anatolia, or, for that matter, Berlin. A border as long as that between Eastern and Western Europe cannot possibly be entirely defensible.

Central Europe—which means Germany—is a different matter. The West certainly disposes of very strong forces to oppose the Warsaw Pact. Manpower figures are always suspect because they depend critically on assumptions about strategic warning, mobilization, and deployments. Nevertheless NATO now has twenty-four divisions in Germany and the low countries facing fifty-seven Pact divisions in East Germany, Poland, and Czechoslovakia—in terms of firepower, one NATO division equalling about three of the Pact's. The tactical-aircraft figures show the West with about 2,800 aircraft in Europe, facing almost 7,000 Pact aircraft of lower, but improving, quality. The Pact enjoys better than a two-to-one superiority in artillery tubes, with artillery of excellent quality. The Pact has a truly formidable advantage in tanks—about 40,000 to one-third as many in the West. Western troops are generally well deployed but not terribly well trained—the United States no longer has a draft to support mobilization, and the period of conscription in the NATO countries is so short that the troops get little training. U.S. forces generally have artillery and logistical support for about thirty days; our allies are reported to have less. The Warsaw Pact has plenty of problems of its own, such as the steady deterioration in the quality of the Soviet conscript and the unreliability of the Pact troops, particularly the Poles. But two-thirds of the Pact divisions, tanks, and aircraft are Soviet; the units are usually combat-ready and at full strength, and the perceived qualitative advantages of Western arms are vanishing. Each side has its major doctrinal drawbacks. NATO forces are saddled with a doctrine of forward defense that precludes their falling back to use the Rhine as a natural barrier. Furthermore, NATO is truly a multinational force, requiring effective coordination of forces of multiple countries to be effective. Neither the Americans nor the Germans can rely just on their own forces and tactics if war comes. The Pact forces are overwhelmingly Soviet, with a strong German component, simplifying problems of language and training, but the Soviets must send troops and supplies through Poland, using Polish troops for combat support. If the Pact were attacked, the Poles would probably support the Soviets; but if the attack came from the East, who could tell?

The West can hardly be sanguine about the picture painted here. The best that can be said is that in absolute terms, the forces arrayed in or available to both sides in Germany are very large and very strong, though the relative advantage must go to the Pact. The Pact could not count on a quick breakthrough and would be likely to find a nonnuclear war lasting a long time and, therefore, bearing great risk of escalation to one of the higher levels of violence involving nuclear weapons. Nevertheless, the West must conclude that its forces do not promise success in a nonnuclear war; NATO counts on risk, political considerations, and nuclear weapons to deter nonnuclear war in Central Europe, and lacks a credible threat to start the massive use of nonnuclear forces against the Pact, in response to, say, an attack in Norway or a provocation in Yugoslavia.

Even more worrisome than the static balance of forces in Central Europe is the trend in these forces. Starting from an already high base in 1975, by 1981 the Soviets had effectively doubled the number of tanks in Europe, while the United States stayed constant and our European allies increased their tanks by only 20 percent. Similarly, artillery in NATO has remained nearly constant, while Pact artillery increased 75 percent. The buildup in Pact airpower, while not serious in numbers, has seen significant modernization.

In short, Western commanders in Europe command very strong conventional forces, but face even stronger forces across the border that have been growing and improving at a worrisome rate. What is particularly puzzling is the rationale behind the extended, continuing Soviet buildup. On the one hand, a battlefield bristling with both conventional and nuclear forces can hardly offer a Soviet commander an encouraging prospect for a safe aggression; on the other, Soviet forces (and those of the rest of the Pact) are much more than adequate to deter or counter any attack on the part of the West. In any event, looking at the forces in Europe, a prudent military strategist would conclude that (1) NATO does not have a credible ability to threaten to use its conventional forces except in self-defense, and (2) although its conventional defense is much more than a tripwire, if NATO is attacked its conventional defense would be likely either to fail or to stall, and NATO would need to resort to nuclear weapons.

Consideration of chemical weapons adds to the uneasiness on the NATO side. The principal military impact of the threatened use of chemical weapons is the need to employ defensive measures—airtight suits, masks, and gloves—that greatly hinder the ability of soldiers to perform their tasks. Pact forces are equipped with and regularly train with chemical weapons, while NATO is limited to defensive chemical measures. The ability of Pact forces to employ chemical weapons as part of an offensive thrust would put NATO troops at an important disadvantage, while NATO has neither the chemical weapons nor the doctrine to force the choice of the time and place. NATO must, in fact, rely on the threat of nuclear weapons to deter the Pact from using chemicals.

The Effect on the Balance of Introducing Battlefield Nuclear Weapons

If there were a ground war in Central Europe, one has to conclude that there is a high probability that battlefield nuclear weapons would be employed. First of all Soviet doctrine and, more importantly, Soviet exercises seem to suggest a dependence on combined-arms warfare using conventional, chemical, and nuclear forces from the start. Furthermore, even a war that started on a conventional level would likely force the West to consider nuclear weapons or to suffer major losses, as discussed earlier.

U.S. and Soviet strategies for battlefield nuclear weapons differ quite significantly. Most U.S. battlefield weapons are low-yield and are coupled to relatively short-range delivery systems—primarily tube artillery. These weapons represent an extension of conventional firepower, requiring an ability to acquire individual battlefield targets and to hit these targets accurately. This strategy is a reasonable one for forces that are trying to protect their own lands without killing their own civilians and destroying their own property. Soviet tactical-nuclear strategy, on the other hand, is built around battlefield missiles delivering much higher-yield weapons in lethal attacks on large areas, rather than on specific targets. This strategy does not require detailed battlefield intelligence and, if employed in a country as crowded as the Federal Republic, would lead to massive civilian casualties and destruction. In both strategies, the objective is to destroy the ground forces of the enemy and allow a rapid decisive attack (or counterattack) before the enemy could replace its massive losses with fresh troops. NATO has 4,000–5,000 nuclear-artillery rounds—the Soviets have perhaps 10 percent as many; but the Pact enjoys a marked advantage in battlefield nuclear missiles.

There is no experience to guide us in analyzing a war involving battlefield nuclear weapons, so analysts should be even more cautious than usual. Nevertheless it appears that NATO could have little confidence that the first use of battlefield nuclear weapons would redound to its advantage. NATO's only real hope would be to use them so massively and with such surprise that they could annihilate Pact forces before these could retaliate in kind. However, given the short ranges and low yields of most of NATO's battlefield nuclear weapons, the risk of collateral damage if used in the Federal Republic, and problems in keeping secrets from the Soviets, this event does appear unlikely. In this context enhanced-radiation (ER) warheads on Lance missiles do appear to be important militarily. The relatively long range of Lance—on the order of 200 kilometers—coupled with the ability of the radiation warheads to kill large numbers of armored and mechanized troops without enormous collateral damage, would permit NATO commanders some hope of an effective nuclear counterstroke in a desperate situation.

In the absence of extended-radiation weapons, it appears that introduction of battlefield nuclear weapons would work to the disadvantage of NATO. Whereas NATO's conventional prospects are not encouraging, they are at least serious and would have to be heavily considered by Soviet planners. The introduction of battlefield nuclear weapons, *even if NATO used them first*, would almost certainly disadvantage NATO (in the absence of large stocks of ER weapons on longer-range delivery systems that could blanket the approach and staging areas in East Germany) because the remaining higher yield, longer-range Soviet weapons would still be lethal to NATO troops. The risk that battlefield nuclear weapons may be used out of desperation, coupled with uncertainties as to where these might lead, can probably continue to be a major part of an overall deterrent strategy, but to an analyst the threat or use of battlefield nuclear weapons promises only disadvantage to NATO.

Long-Range-Theater Nuclear Forces

If NATO commanders are faced with uncertain prospects for nonnuclear warfare and positively discouraging prospects for the introduction of battlefield nuclear weapons, then the next question is what solace might they find in forces at the next level of violence—long-range theater nuclear forces?

Before addressing that question one must first address the question of the roles of LRTNF. One possible role would be as a credible, last-ditch deterrent to an otherwise successful, nonnuclear or battlefield-nuclear-aided Pact attack on Western Europe. In this context, the combination of strong conventional forces, battlefield nuclear forces, and LRTNF is supposed to present the Pact with the following prospects: Sucess of a nonnuclear attack was not assured, and introduction of battlefield weapons would be so destructive that NATO would have little further incentive not to use LRTNF against the USSR and therefore the risk of attacking Western Europe would outweigh the potential gain.

The problem with this line of reasoning is that a LRTNF attack on the USSR would lead to such a powerful response of SS–20s and Backfires that Western Europe losses would far outweigh Soviet losses. Nevertheless as the number of LRTNF in Western Europe increase, the possibility of very severe damage to the USSR increases. From this point of view, what appears to be important is the absolute level of destructiveness of LRTNF based in Western Europe, primarily in Germany. According to this argument, in the absence of NATO LRTNF forces, the Soviets might act as if they could attack Western Europe and, win or lose, be fairly sure that the USSR will remain a sanctuary because U.S.-based forces would be deterred from attacking. This line of reasoning grants that the USSR can destroy Western Europe but hopes that it will not do so—for why destroy what you wish to capture? It is hard to see what credibility the British strike forces would add, whereas the value of the French forces would depend on the scenario.

The second role of LRTNF is to counter Soviet threats of using their own weapons—SS–4s, SS–5s, SS–20s and Backfires—against Western Europe in the absence of a ground attack. The fear here is that the USSR could exact benefit through such threats to Western Europe, while the U.S. vulnerability to strategic attack would vitiate the power of the U.S.-based forces to deter such Soviet threats. LRTNF arms control measures are primarily oriented towards this role. In the extreme, if all LRTNF on both sides were neutralized, this role would disappear. Thus, once LRTNF levels are high enough to remove the Soviets' prospects of home sanctuary in an attack on Western Europe, even higher levels of LRTNF can be fruitfully traded for reductions in Soviet forces targeted on Western Europe.

Military Factors in Europe

Recap from the Top Down

NATO long-range theater nuclear forces play two roles: threat to the Soviet homeland as an ultimate deterrent to a large-scale Warsaw Pact invasion of Western Europe, and as a theater-based deterrent to Soviet threats to use their own LRTNF against Western Europe. The scenario underlying the first role is that a Warsaw Pact invasion could be so devastating and so successful, that NATO Europe has little more to lose in threatening or attacking the USSR. Almost by definition, no level of Soviet LRTNF would suffice to deter a NATO threat in this scenario. The important point is that NATO conventional and battlefield nuclear forces must be strengthened such that no Pact *blitzkrieg* could succeed. As long as the Pact is face with all-out war or failure, the NATO-LRTNF strike is a credible part of the deterrent. This consideration is little affected by recent Soviet increases in SS–20s and Backfires, since additional Soviet Eurostrategic forces would be unlikely to deter the West from such a last-ditch threat. Much more worrisome is the continuing buildup in Soviet conventional forces, which could perhaps achieve their objectives so quickly that the NATO-LRTNF threat would be meaningless.

The second role of NATO LRTNF is to counter Soviet threats of using their Eurostrategic forces against Western Europe. This is the context in which the buildup of SS–20s and Backfires is most meaningful. The lower that LRTNF levels in Europe can be set, the better that this Soviet threat can be countered. Since in this role LRTNF are not tied to a ground battle, all theater forces (and not just those from the countries whose territory is at risk), including British, French, and U.S. sea-based forces in the Mediterranean, ought to be considered as parts of the equation.

3 Allies, Angst, and Arms Control: New Troubles for an Old Partnership

Josef Joffe

From MLF to INF

Transatlantic doubts and debates about nuclear strategy have always been about politics. This is the central paradox of the postwar-security relationship between the United States and Europe. As we look at the widening fissures engendered by intermediate-nuclear force (INF) modernization and arms control, fissures that have opened within societies as well as between allies, we might do well to recall the events of almost twenty years ago when the last attempt at countering the Soviet missile threat against Europe was launched and finally scuttled.

Twenty years ago, the Multilateral Force (MLF) raised a good many of the painful issues unsettling the alliance today. Although the MLF was ostensibly designed to address a strategic problem (Soviet medium-range ballistic missiles (MRBMs) deployed against Western Europe), it was at heart a political instrument of American diplomacy. Set in motion to allay European security concerns regarding the Soviet bloc, the missile-bearing fleet ended up provoking the most fearful disputes about power and paramountcy in the Western camp. In the process, the MLF provided an instructive case study in irony: solutions dramatized dilemmas; unifying moves deepened dissension; American accommodation to presumed European wishes spawned resentment and hostility among America's allies.

Reading an early postmortem of the MLF impresses the present-day reader with a haunting sense of deja vu. "The original proposal for a NATO multilateral force," wrote Henry Kissinger, a prominent student of the project, in 1965,

> grew out of a military "requirement" which had been generated in accordance with the NATO doctrine prevalent in the late fifties. According to this concept, SACEUR was to have the capability to destroy all weapons aimed at Europe. Thus when the Soviet Union began to deploy large numbers of medium-range ballistic missiles in western Russia, two NATO requirements emerged: a modernization program to replace vulnerable tactical aircraft with missiles and an interdiction mission giving NATO the capability to destroy the Soviet MRBMs.[1]

When a partial plan was first put forward by the Kennedy administration, "it did not elicit a significant European response." Nor was it, at this point "a high priority goal of American foreign policy."[2] The project assumed urgency only after French President de Gaulle, in his notorious press conference of January 14, 1963, vetoed Britain's application to the European Economic Community while heaping scorn on the very idea of nuclear integration. The MLF was infused with new vigor, but not because the strategic facts had suddenly changed. Ironically, "until six weeks before it emerged as a principal objective of American NATO policy, our highest officials had declared the MLF militarily necessary."[3] The MLF was activated because de Gaulle had issued his strongest-ever challenge to American hegemony at the same time that he was multiplying his efforts in the transatlantic tug-of-war for Germany's allegiance.

"If de Gaulle meant to make West Germany choose between France and the United States," an inside chronicler of the Kennedy administration noted, "the MLF, in Washington's view, was the way to make it clear that Bonn would find greater security in the Atlantic relationship.[4] The many-flagged fleet was thus set on a strictly political course, turning into a multipurpose diplomatic instrument. It was designed to harness Germany's presumed nuclear ambitions to a collective enterprise (under American control). It was to discourage the allies from following England's and France's lead into their own quest for a national deterrent. It was supposed to bridge the status gap between the alliance's nuclear haves and have-nots. In short, the MLF was to enhance centralized American control over nuclear weapons under the guise of sharing them, since Washington's veto on the actual use of the seaborne missiles was to be retained under all circumstances.

Given its political thrust, the MLF's strategic rationale remained in the dark—and mercifully so. The project raised many more problems than it could possibly solve. If the MLF's Polaris missiles were to generate a counterforce capability, why were only 200 projected? At this point, the Soviets had already deployed some 600 MRBMs against Western Europe; they could hardly be eliminated with a puny missile force a third as large. Yet if the MLF projectiles could achieve this task only in conjunction with the U.S. Strategic Air Command (SAC), why have two nuclear strike forces in the alliance—especially if both would remain under American control? If the new missiles were to lighten the burden of deterrence then carried by vulnerable strike aircraft, why put them on vulnerable surface ships? And if the MLF were to increase the credibility of extended deterrence by somehow integrating the European allies, why the insistence on an undiluted American veto? If the American president remained in charge, it was by no means self-evident that he would more readily launch a Polaris located on an MLF freighter off the European coast than the same missile located on an American submarine somewhere in the oceans. And if Washington were ever to relinquish its veto as some American officials were then hinting—the prospect was clearly absurd. It would have meant that the United States would either go to war with a very small poriton of its nuclear arsenal (while holding back its SAC forces) or conversely throw everything into the battle, yet neither as result of a national decision, but rather in response to an Allied majority vote.

Luckily, these questions were never debated, luckily the MLF sank in the crossfire of political dissension before it could dramatize all the irreducible dilemmas embodied in a strategic doctrine erected on the uncertain premise of extended deterrence. The British remained politely indifferent. The French escalated their hostility as the Americans increased their pressure, and the smaller allies dropped out one by one. It was only in Germany that lukewarm interest changed into avid support. The transformation was preceded by a fierce domestic battle between Atlanticists and Gaullists (within the ruling CDU/CSU Party alignment). The day was carried by the Atlanticists around Chancellor Ludwig Erhard, yet the victory proved an empty one.

In the first place, Bonn's mounting attachment to the MLF (in the end only the Germans and the Americans were still committed to the project) was almost identical with its death knell. Among Bonn's allies this turn of events raised the specter of too much of a German say in matters nuclear (in a German-American axis) when most of them had warily gone along in order to prevent such increase. Secondly, once the Atlanticists had proven victorious at home (summer 1964) and once the Federal Republic loosened de Gaulle's embrace and returned to the American fold, the MLF was no longer necessary. Finally, American global interests began to shift—toward limited collaboration with the Soviet Union as exemplified by the Non-Proliferation Treaty (NPT) and toward escalation in Vietnam. By early 1965, the MLF was effectively scuttled.

From MLF to INF: *Le Plus ça Change*

The doctrinal questions raised by the MLF have not disappeared. Indeed the quantum jump embodied in the deployment of Soviet second-generation Eurostrategic forces has merely dramatized the problems of yore; nor have the peculiar interaction patterns between the United States and Europe fundamentally changed. When it comes to matters nuclear, the pattern is one of perversity: bargaining and negotiation across the Atlantic does not result in rapprochment; instead, a curious minuet-like mating dance occurs where both sides merely shift their positions 180 degrees. As a result, they remain as far apart as before.

The story of INF modernization has the same beginning as that of the Multilateral Force. Whether it will have the same ending is as yet unclear.

By the mid-seventies, the two key strategic issues were again vulnerability and counterforce. (Only the labels had changed slightly: to survivability and penetrability.) While Soviet capabilities were improving rapidly in terms of numbers, accuracy, and mobility, Western LRTNF were just as rapidly approaching obsolescence. In NATO, the main load of Eurostrategic deterrence was being carried by strike aircraft such as the Starfighter and Vulcan, which were first deployed in 1958 and 1960. They were based on airfields that were destined to be the prime targets of a preemptive attack, and if they did survive, they ran a diminishing chance of penetrating because of the Warsaw Pact's increasing investment in air defenses. In short, something had to be done about the survivability and penetrability of NATO's LRTNF (as well as about endangered C^3 links).

A key sentence in the communique of the Nuclear Planning Group, meeting in Brussels in June 1975, referred to the "continuing examination of the implications of technological improvements which might affect NATO's deterrent posture . . . and nuclear defense capabilities.[5] This barren phrase concealed a miracle weapon—the cruise missile—which soon came to be regarded as a panacea for almost all of NATO's strategic ills. In theory, it was mobile enough to be all but invulnerable. It could not only fly farther than existing LRTNF, it could also penetrate the densest air-defense network and still hit remote targets with unprecedented precision. The cruise missile offered the best of all possible deterrence worlds: precise enough to be a counterforce weapon, not fast enough to pose a first-strike threat.

It posed no political problems for the Allies, Europeans as well as Americans, until 1977. At the beginning of that year, however, Jimmy Carter and Harold Brown replaced Gerald Ford and James Schlesinger, both active supporters of TNF modernization with cruise missiles. The West German strategist Uwe Nerlich thinks that "INF modernization would have proceeded within the normal bureaucratic channels under the old administration. Yet Jimmy Carter brought an anti-nuclear 'theology' to the White House which regarded cruise missiles as veritable anathema of arms control."[6]

Given the new mood in Washington, conflict with the European allies was now practically foreordained—all the more so because the Soviet Union was adamantly pressuring the administration to accept stringent range limitations for GLCMs, as well as noncircumvention clauses in the context of SALT II. This led to a first, albeit muted, warning by West German Chancellor Helmut Schmidt in the fall of 1977:

> SALT neutralizes (the superpowers') strategic nuclear capabilities. In Europe this magnifies the significance of the disparities between East and West in nuclear, tactical and conventional weapons. . . . We in Europe must be particularly careful that these (superpower) negotiations do not neglect the components of NATO's deterrent strategy. . . . Strategic arms limitations confined to the United States and the Soviet Union will inevitably impair the security of the West European members of the Alliance vis-a-vis Soviet military superiority in Europe if we do not succeed in removing the disparities

of military power in Europe parallel to the SALT negotiations. So long as this is not the case we must maintain the balance of the full range of deterrence strategy. *The Alliance must, therefore, be ready to make available the means to support the present strategy.*[7]

By December 1977, Defense Minister Georg Leber was already expressing West German concerns a good deal more bluntly. Where Schmidt had called attention mainly to the growing disparities on the Eurostrategic level (while remaining ambiguous about the policy implications), his defense minister came out clearly for compensatory rearmament. Moreover, he proclaimed publicly that SALT must not foreclose a cruise-missile option for the European allies.[8] And if there had to be a range limit for GLCMs, 1500 kilometers were far more appropriate than the 600 kilometers, which were ultimately enshrined in the Protocol.

At this point, the West Germans in particular had become noticeably nervous. Given Jimmy Carter's stake in a SALT II agreement, they worried not about too little detente (as today) but about too much—about the kind of Big Two cordiality that might sacrifice West European strategic needs on the altar of superpower arms control. For the West Germans, Jimmy Carter's priorities were obviously askew. While his emissaries toured Europe throughout 1977 and 1978 pushing conventional modernization of NATO forces, his Secretary of Defense Harold Brown kept proclaiming that the U.S. retaliatory potential was large enough to counter not only the "central balance" arsenal of the Soviets but also their Eurostrategic potential.[9]

In other words, at this juncture the Germans were the *demandeurs*, and the Americans were at best lukewarm to the idea of LRTNF modernization. For both, the issue was again at heart a political one. The Carter administration wanted a SALT II agreement as visible testimony to its quest for global arms control. For the Germans, cruise missiles assumed (true to deeply entrenched historical patterns) a symbolic quality—as measure of the reliability of the American commitment to German security and to German interests.[10]

Subsequently, however, both sides were to shift course by 180 degrees—and both in response to profound political changes at home. In Bonn (as throughout most of northern Europe) the transformation was triggered by the neutron bomb—the enhanced radiation warhead—which was broached as an addition to American arsenals in Europe. It was never added but its political impact was so enormous that it changed all the political equations in West Germany. By the time Jimmy Carter had "postponed" an American-production decision in April of 1978, the policymakers in Bonn had been forced to realize that their margin of maneuver in matters nuclear had shrunken drastically—under the double impact of popular revulsion at home and Soviet pressures from abroad.

In the meantime, the Carter administration was also faced by a fronde at home—except that it marched to a totally different drumbeat. Given the mounting opposition to SALT II in the Senate and society at large, Carter and his cohorts realized that their arms-control policy could only be saved at the rice of more arms—be it the MX or medium-range missiles in Europe. By early 1979, the administration finally came around to granting their allies the hardware that they had so long cherished in vain. Alas, too late: Helmut Schmidt, who in the fall of 1977 was the first Western statesman to sound the alarm, now confronted a deeply entrenched opposition in his own party that regarded INF modernization as the deathblow to Ostpolitik and detente with the Soviets.[11]

Helmut Schmidt was thus forced into the obverse of Carter's tactics: He could save TNF modernization only at the price of disarmament. Hence, the two-track decision fathered by the German chancellor (Schmidt: "I was one of the authors") and ratified several months later by NATO in Brussels on December 12, 1979. Arms control talks with the USSR became the precondition, alibi, or substitute for what the Germans now called *Nachrustung* (compensatory arming) rather than modernization. Or as the last sentence of the Brussels decision put it: "The TNF needs of NATO will be examined in the light of concrete negotiation results."[12]

INF Modernization and Arms Control:
The Ascendency of Domestic Politics

The preceding survey suggests that, throughout the past quarter century, it was political rather than military needs that shaped nuclear choices on both sides of the Atlantic—more often than not without due regard to the needs and sensitivites of allies. Yet there is a limit to the lessons of history. Even if the MLF and INF complexes share many similarities (stemming from the built-in nuclear dilemmas of the Alliance), there is one key difference between the 1960s and 1980s that might end up twisting the analogies out of shape completely: domestic politics.

The MLF episode was a classic interstate affair. The main actors were governments whose interests converged, changed, and collided. If domestic politics did enter into the balance, it did so in a highly structured fashion. In the United States, for instance, the peculiarities of intrabureaucratic rivalry go some way toward explaining why and when the MLF was pushed to the fore, then ultimately sunk. In West Germany, the growing infatuation with the missile fleet was closely linked to the rise and eventual resolution of the intraparty power struggle between Atlanticists and Gaullists within the ruling CDU/CSU alignment.

The TNF drama, however, has been unfolding on a thoroughly transformed stage. In Europe, particularly in the pivotal country Germany, the impact of domestic politics has been direct, unfiltered, inchoate. The government is holding on bravely, but its control seems to be slipping. The Social Democratic

Party which started out by successfully enveloping the antimodernization forces in the tenuous compromise of the two-track decision, is now deeply rent. Worse, it is threatened on its left by an amorphous, but burgeoning, grass-roots movement without a defined structure or accepted leaders. Its aims are unclear, ranging from the limited objective of preventing an LRTNF deployment via neutralism to unilateral disarmament. Its membership is motley, including pastors and pacifists, Jusos and Judos, ex–party leaders and exgenerals, Christians and Communists.[13] And its methods have clearly transcended the entrenched routines of traditional party politics. The thrust is plebiscitary, the instruments are appeals and signature collections, marches and demonstrations. To simplify at the risk of crudeness: In West Germany the issue may no longer be whether the government (and the SPD) can stick to the finely (perhaps too finely) balanced two-track decision, but whether they can channel and control the peace movement over the next two or three years.[14]

What holds true for West Germany, holds true for most of Northern Europe. As a perceptive British observer recently put it, "Pandora's Box has been opened. For good or ill, nuclear strategy in Europe has been a 'leadership decision', taken by an informed few—a tiny nuclear elite—on behalf of an only-intermittently-interested many. . . . That no longer applies in Western Europe. The Pandora's Box of the nuclear age is public participation in nuclear policy-making; and the true message of the protest movements . . . is that the lid has opened."[15]

Where participation on previously arcane issues becomes public, moods matter. By "mood" I mean the raw substratum of politics: a society's basic perceptions and assumptions, its fears and ambitions, its sense of itself and the world at large. And at this point, it is quite obvious that national moods on the opposite shores of the ocean are sorely out of phase. Indeed, it is hard to recall a previous period in the history of the alliance when our moods were as incongruent as they are today.

As Western Europe (with the occasional exception of France in Shaba and England in the Falklands) holds fast to the comforts of an insular existence, the United States has begun to shed its Vietnam-based inhibitions and to strike out for a "can do," even neonationalist role in the world. If Europeans cling to the status quo, Americans seem eager to change it. While Europe's populations are increasingly awed (some would even say terrorized) by the prospect of crisis and war, American society, reacting to a sense of earlier weakness, seems prepared to underwrite a massive arms buildup as key to an activist policy of neocontainment.

Europeans are prone to regard armament efforts as provocation and arms control as an end in itself; Americans tend to view arms control as a past gateway for Soviet opportunism and rearmament as prime guarantee for future Soviet restraint. In a policy context, Europeans and Americans tend to look at

Figure 3–1. The Pershing II

arms and arms control as means toward quite disparate ends. After Afghanistan and the Ayatollah, Americans have asked how arms and arms control affect our security. Europeans ask how they affect their political relation with the Soviet Union and Eastern Europe.

With regard to INF arms control, the differences are no less palpable. For many West Europeans, INF talks look as if they are a good way of avoiding a INF build-up; for many Americans INF talks seem to be an unavoidable concession on the road to the deployment of Pershing II and Tomahawk.

Throughout the first year of its existence, the Reagan administration remained blissfully oblivious to the climate of sheer angst spreading through Europe. Each time Haig, Weinberger, and Reagan speculated in public about the likelihood of a nuclear war limited to Europe, the peace movement added new recruits to its cause. By October 1981, hundreds of thousands of demonstrators were gathering in the capitals of Western Europe to protest against Pershing and GLCM, some of them even against the very alliance that had protected the peace for over thirty years. By November, the Reagan administration had finally realized that the rhetoric of resolve would hardly win the battle for the "hearts and minds" of its European allies. Neatly sidestepping all the intractable issues that had bedeviled the alliance's LRTNF posture since the mid-seventies, Ronald Reagan thus came forward with a bold arms control proposal—the zero option. Paying homage to the concerns of Europe's young, he vowed: "The United States is prepared to cancel its deployment of Pershing II and ground-launched cruise missiles if the Soviets will dismantle their SS–20, SS–4, and SS–5 missiles."[16]

The new tone evidently reflected the conviction that the United States can—and must—influence the climate of the European INF debate. Similarly, President Reagan's speech in May 1982, where he proposed deep cuts in the number of strategic warheads "by at least a third below current levels,"[17] was directed as much against the European peace movement as against the American freeze movement.

Both moves made political sense. Where previously arcane issues such as LRTNF are thrashed out in the streets, nuclear strategy becomes a subspecies of domestic politics. Where the din of demonstrations drowns out the reasoned analysis of strategic needs and options, the premium is on quick "P.R. fixes" and newsworthy propaganda victories. From about 1978 to 1982, this problem used to be strictly European; the sudden rise of the American peace movement in early 1982 made sure that strategy-as-domestic-politics would now be played out in the vastness of the transatlantic arena. As a result, governments on both sides of the Atlantic were even less likely to address the two central alliance questions of the 1980s: Why do we want to modernize our nuclear arsenals? Why, and to which end, do we want to negotiate about arms control?

Paying homage to the sensitivites to America's allies, as Reagan did in his zero-option speech, will at least lower the temperatures and undercut those

Figure 3–2. Ground-Launched Cruise Missile

who use American "war mongering" as convenient pretext for a wholesale attack against the U.S. presence in Europe and the very idea of alliance. Moderate rhetoric and supple diplomacy will also lighten the task of governments that—rightly or wrongly—believe that they are the prisoners of domestic opinion. Finally, less heat and more light might have a decisive impact on the margin which, in democracies, is often decisive.

Conversely, if we do not succeed in lowering the temperatures, we might end up with the worst of all possible worlds: with neither modernization nor arms control, for if European governments in the northern tier became convinced that they cannot neutralize the opposition, the USSR's incentive for serious INF negotiations will surely vanish. Why bargain if there is no price attached to inaction?

Yet a more moderate climate will not solve the problem of European security in the 1980s and beyond. The problem is extended deterrence in an age of parity. The problem is a surfeit of (short-range and high-yield) battlefield weapons that mainly threaten their users, and a shortage of longer-range INF that satisfy the two key requirements of deterrence: invulnerability and penetrability. The problem, finally, is an arms control design—the zero option—which might remove only part of the Soviet threat while keeping the West from modernizing the most crucial part of its Euronuclear arsenal. Almost twenty years after the sinking of MLF we are back to where we started.

The problems, in detail, are these:

1. On the Warsaw Pact side, there is a superabundance of LRTNF. Even a cautious estimate like the IISS *Military Balance 1981/82* specifies some 2000 nuclear warheads that the Soviet Union can hurl into Western Europe by rocket or plane. Since NATO only offers a few hundred strategically relevant targets, these assets represent an impressive overkill capacity.
2. NATO's long-range nuclear sword has been blunted. Its cutting edge is represented by aging fighter bombers such as the F–104 Starfighter, the F–4 Phantom, the British Vulcan, the French Mirage IV, and the American F–111 The F–111 is the most "modern" addition to the Alliance's LRTNF arsenal; it was first stationed in England in 1967. Its European counterparts such as the Starfighter and the Vulcan, were first deployed in 1958 and 1960; both are on the way to the scrap heap. In addition, these planes are concentrated in a few vulnerable air bases which represent first-class first-strike targets. And if they ever do take off, their chances of actually penetrating to their targets in the East are rapidly diminishing, since the Warsaw Pact is covered by one of the densest air-defense networks in the world.
3. Those NATO warheads that are delivered by rocketry or artillery contribute mainly to *self*-deterrence. The majority of the alliance's so-called tactical weapons threaten our own population because 60 percent of the total have a range of under twenty-five kilometers.
4. Those battlefield weapons, the lowest rung of the escalation ladder, are extremely vulnerable because they are concentrated in about fifty bases. If they are not destroyed by Warsaw Pact missiles, they might be easily overrun by the first wave of an attack. Given the complicated chain of

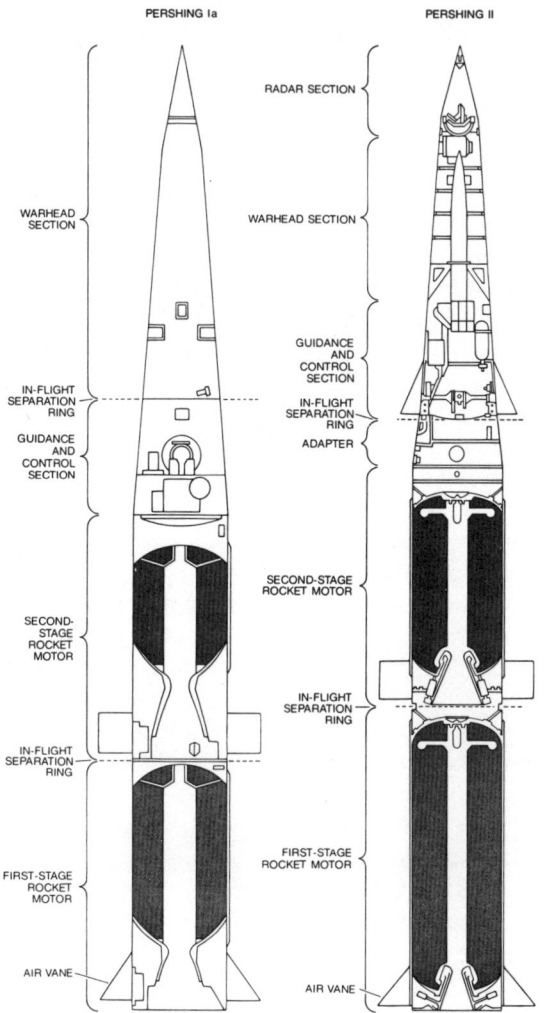

Figure 3-3. Pershing II and Pershing I Compared

Source: Kevin N. Lewis "Intermediate-Range Nuclear Weapons," *Scientific America*. December 1980, p. 2.

Pershing II, the new U.S. intermediate-range ballistic missiles scheduled for deployment with the forces of the North Atlantic Treaty Organization in Western Europe, is compared here with the missile it would replace, the Pershing Ia. Both missiles are designed to be fired from mobile field launchers and both have a solid-fuel two-stage propulsion system. The advanced terminal-guidance system of the Pershing II, however, makes it much more accurate than its inertially guided predecessor. The improvement in accuracy has made it possible to greatly reduce the explosive yield of the new missile's nuclear warhead, creating more room for fuel and helping to increase the weapon's range: from approximately 650 kilometers for the Pershing Ia to 1,800 kilometers for the Pershing II (long enough to reach the USSR).

command from the field commander through the U.S. president, there is a hiatus of up to twenty-four hours before authorization travels back to the frontline troops.
5. Finally, and this is the most grotesque implication of President Reagan's zero option offered, the USSR could easily dispense with all of its SS-4, SS-5, and SS-20 without losing its Eurostrategic edge. In the first place, the Soviets are taking out reinsurance elsewhere by deploying the successor generation SS-21, SS-22, and SS-23. Their range is between 120 and 1000 kilometers. They are two to three times more precise than their predecessors Frog, Scaleboard, and Scud. If deployed forward, in the GDR or in the CSSR, they can cover an arc from Birmingham to Bari, and within this arc, there are most of NATO's strategic targets. In addition, the Warsaw Pact holds a two-to-one superiority in fighter bombers (with a range up to 1000 kilometers).

After a survey of NATO's theater nuclear forces in 1974, former Secretary of Defense James Schlesinger termed the alliance's arsenal "a pile of junk"[18]. Since then, nothing substantial has changed, even though the NATO bureaucracy soon agreed in principle on a comprehensive modernization program that would emphasize mobility, dispersion, fast reaction times, lower yields, greater range, and improved C^3I links. It follows that the zero option can hardly do justice to the strategic problems still facing the Alliance.

Indeed, we cannot even begin to develop a security-improving arms control concept until we first answer a prior question: What is the nature of the threat and the purpose of our forces?

There are at least five rationales for INF modernization:

1. The West must somehow counter the Soviet SS-20 and Backfire buildup. This is the official rationale of the alliance governments.
2. Another rationale concerns selective options: NATO must be able to threaten second- and third-echelon invasion forces without recourse to strategic strikes.
3. A third rationale derives from the problem of vulnerability: NATO must have retaliatory weapons that are hard to preempt, hence mobile and dispersed.
4. A fourth rationale is concerned with extended deterrence and coupling: American LRTNF capable of threatening the Soviet sanctuary must be stationed on the Continent so as to underline strategic homogeneity and the community of fate between the United States and Europe.
5. Finally, as a fifth rationale has it, NATO must regain the escalation dominance implicit in the doctrine of flexible response, now grievously threatened by the Soviet buildup on the strategic as well as continental level.

How, then, does the alliance's Brussels decision of December 1979 relate to these rationales?

1. If the SS–20 is the problem, then 464 slow-flying cruise missiles are not the answer because they cannot fulfill a counterforce mission against mobile MRBMs.
2. If NATO wants to threaten Soviet invasion forces in the rear, then GLCMs are both useful and cost effective. On the other hand, the capabilities of Tomahawk and Pershing II are both excessive and provocative. To threaten the bases and staging areas of the Warsaw Pact requires neither GLCMs with a 2500-kilometer range nor Pershing II with terminal guidance and earth-burrowing capabilities.
3. If the problem is vulnerability, then LRTNF should not be stationed in a few land bases but at sea—preferably in submarines even at the risk of diminished C^3 and targeting precision. Alternatively, GLCMs should be coupled to heavy-load helicopters so as to allow for rapid dispersion in times of crisis.
4. If we want to enhance the credibility of extended deterrence, then land-based systems are indispensable because they would force the Soviets to attack part of the American strategic arsenal in the process of attacking Europe. (Significantly, the Soviets have never drawn a fine distinction between Euro-based and American-based weapons capable of hitting Soviet territory; they regard both as strategic.)
5. Finally, if the issue is escalation dominance, then 572 systems as envisaged in Brussels are far too few.

These are some of the dilemmas besetting NATO's planned LRTNF posture. That they are unresolved is hardly surprising. For at Brussels, the alliance essentially sought to establish a political, not a military, balance; yet unless we tackle these conundrums, we cannot even begin to design an agenda for arms control, to wit:

1. If we continue to focus on the SS–20, we might perhaps be able to negotiate them away (to the scrap heap or just to Siberia?)—only to realize that we have a new problem on our hands: SS–21, SS–22, and SS–23, plus Soviet frontal aviation whose range is sufficiently large to cover most of NATO's worthwhile targets.
2. If we want to threaten Soviet second- and third-echelon forces, we could dispense with swift, terminally guided Pershing II (regarded as a supreme threat by the Soviets) while insisting on the deployment of a credible cruise-missile potential.
3. If our problem is vulnerability, then "it is more important to deploy most or all the GLCMs and Pershings than it is to wrest ten or twenty-percent reductions in the number of SS–20s."[19]

4. If we worry about coupling (as Europeans should), then our arms control agenda must again be quite modest. Extended deterrence requires a highly visible U.S. commitment, hence land-based LRTNF stationed on European soil so as to complicate Soviet calculations. Since the Soviets cannot hope to preempt all of these systems, they must countenance the possibility of being hit in return. If so, they could hardly confine their salvoes to America's Europe-based systems only—aiming, as it were, at their adversary's switchblade while leaving his sword untouched. It follows that the Soviets must attack America's entire panoply. Raising the specter of all-out war, such decision is not lightly taken, and in this chain of calculations lies the very essence of extended deterrence.[20]

5. Finally, if the issue is the end of escalation dominance, then INF talks as currently envisaged are of limited value unless they are integrated in negotiations covering the entire spectrum of nuclear weapons. "It makes little sense to formalize limits on the SS-20 if limits on Soviet ICBMs were in doubt. INF negotiations thus presume *some* shape to SALT."[21] President Reagan's START offer of May 9, 1982, has at least promised an end to the strategic arms control hiatus that began in 1979. Yet SALT II, a rather rudimentary exercise when compared to the TNF-START complex, took almost seven years. How many years will it take to negotiate limits on a gamut of weapons extending from nuclear howitzer shells to Trident, encompassing not only Soviets and Americans, but—directly or indirectly—French, British, Germans, Italians?

Can the alliance afford to do nothing while the talks continue at the leisurely rhythm of, say, the MBFR negotiations in Vienna? Can we afford another MLF? We have shied away from these questions in earlier, more tranquil times. Can we begin to answer them now that the Pandora's box has been opened?

Notes

1. Henry A. Kissinger, *The Troubled Partnership* (New York: McGraw-Hill, 1965), p. 128.
2. Ibid., p. 130, 131.
3. Ibid., p. 141.
4. Arthur Schlesinger, *A Thousand Days* (New York: Fawcett Crest, 1967), p. 744–745.
5. NATO Press Service, "NATO Nuclear Planning Group Communique," (Brussels: June 17, 1975).
6. As quoted in Josef Joffe, "Von der Nachrustung zur Null-Rustung," *Die Zeit* (November 27, 1981). Given their small size and multimode

deployment (nuclear as well as conventional), cruise missiles defied a key cannon of prevailing arms control doctrine: verification by national technical means.

7. "The 1977 Alastair Buchan Memorial Lecture," (October 28, 1977); *Survival* (January/February 1978): 3-4 (emphasis added).

8. In a television interview with Lothar Ruehl during the December 1977 NATO Ministerial Meeting in Brussels. Cf. Lothar Ruehl, "Der Beschlub der NATO zur Einfuhrung nuklearer Mittelstreckenwaffen", Europe-Archiv (4/1980), p. 102.

9. Ibid., p. 104.

10. German nervousness about the United States gains additional weight when placed in the overall context of U.S. foreign policy under Carter. Apart from the TNF problem, there were several other prominent issues that placed considerable strain on the relationship regarding human rights, nuclear exports, and economic policy (that is, American insistence that the Federal Republic inflate its economy to act as locomotive for the rest). German concerns over the continental balance were exacerbated further by PRM–10 in 1977, a Presidential Review Memorandum that suggested that NATO troops might have to fall back to the Rhine before regrouping for a counterattack on Warsaw Pact invasion troops.

11. By the beginning of 1979, the antimodernization movement was no longer spearheaded by the left-wing fringe of the SPD but by one of the party's foremost leaders, Herbert Wehner. Unable to sway Schmidt and his new defense minister Hans Spel *in camera,* Wehner took his cause to the media in a series of well-timed interviews. In a talk with the *Neue Ruhr-Zeitung* (January 31, 1979) he declared: "I want to help prevent a drop in the political temperature between the Soviet Union and the West European nations, in particular the Federal Republic, below the freezing point. What we have tried so hard to develop in the past ten years—a contractual relationship—ought not to be destroyed by a lack of patience in regard to disarmament talks." In an interview with the Dutch *NRC Handelsblad* (February 3, 1979) he warned darkly: "This new weapon (Pershing II) signifies an American-West German axis. And this is impossible!"

12. *Bulletin der Bundesregierung,* no. 154 (December 18, 1979) 1410.

13. The Jusos (Young Socialists) and Judos (Young Democrats) are the youth wings of the Social Democratic and Free Democratic parties.

14. Those partial to the search for historical analogies will have to go beyond the MLF to the antinuclear movement of 1958, which sprang up in response to Konrad Adenauer's decision to equip the Bundeswehr with tactical-nuclear launchers and American-controlled warheads. During the first half of 1958, hundreds of thousands took to the streets. Yet by the summer of 1958, the grass roots had wilted as a result of three factors: The SPD was in firm control of the movement; the party was turning sharply right at this point (toward the Atlanticist, anti-Marxist policy embodied in the famous Bad Godesberg program); and the overall political mood in West Germany was

decidedly anti-Communist and pro-American. None of these three factors obtains today.

15. John Barry, "Just Who Is Deterred By The Deterrent?", *The Times* (August 18, 1981), p. 12.

16. Ronald Reagan, "U.S. Program for Peace and Arms Control" *Current Policy* Bureau of Public Affairs, U.S. Department of State, no. 346 (November 18, 1981).

17. Address to the Graduating Class at Eureka College, May 9, 1982. *Wireless Bulletin* (May 10, 1982).

18. As reported by Donald Cotter in an interview with the author. Quoted in Josef Joffe, "Nachtustung zur Null-Rustung".

19. Gregory Treverton, *Nuclear Weapons in Europe,* Adelphi Papers, no. 168 (1981): p. 17.

20. Curiously, the Soviets seem to understand this logic better than does the European peace movement, which has attacked INF modernization as an American conspiracy designed to turn the Continent into a "shooting gallery of the superpowers." Thus a recent Soviet propaganda brochure explains: "It ought to be quite clear that ... any preemptive strike (against Europe) is senseless unless it destroys or at least substantially weakens the *strategic nuclear potential* (emphasis added) of the other side's retaliatory capability ... A first strike in Western Europe would have no sense from any point of view, for it would only expose our country to riposte by an absolutely intact U.S. strategic arsenal." *The Threat to Peace* (Moscow: Progress, 1981), p. 20.

21. Gregory Treverton, ibid., p. 20.

Long-Range-Theater Nuclear Forces in Europe: The Primacy of Politics

Andrew J. Pierre

Political considerations have been, currently are, and surely will continue to be at the root of decisions involving the deployment of American long-range nuclear weapons in Western Europe. This was the case with the introduction and the withdrawal of Thors and Jupiters in the 1950s, the heated debate over the Multilateral Force in the 1960s, and the decision to deploy Tomahawk ground-launched cruise missiles (GLCMs) and Pershing II ballistic missiles in December 1979. The reason is basic: American nuclear weapons in Europe serve the purpose of increasing the credibility of the U.S. security guarantee. From the perspective of the West Europeans, these weapons are designed to ensure that the Soviets know that, before they can conquer Europe, they must face U.S. nuclear weapons. Within the spectrum of nuclear weapons, long-range weapons (defined here as those capable of reaching the Soviet Union from Western Europe—and the reverse) are especially sensitive. It is these weapons that are perceived by some as most certain to couple the defense of Europe with the security of the United States and by others as making possible a war limited to Soviet and European territory, excluding the American homeland. Immediately, we are in the world of political perceptions—and ambiguity.

The military changes that occurred in the strategic balance during the 1970s are not in much dispute; it is the consequences of these changes, as perceived, that are the subject of disagreement. Within the past decade the Soviet Union has achieved rough parity with the United States in central-strategic systems. Second, it has modernized its theater nuclear forces through a program of substituting mobile SS–20 IRBMs with three MIRV warheads for the existing SS–4s and SS–5s. The SS–20s are more accurate and have a more extended range then their predecessors; they are complemented by the deployment of Backfire bombers. Third, and less noticed, there has been a substantial modernization of shorter-range Soviet theater nuclear forces. These include missile launchers with Soviet combat troops in Eastern Europe, nuclear–capable artillery, and an array of strike fighters and medium bombers capable of reaching well into Western Europe.

For some observers, the emergence of parity throws into grave doubt the credibility of the American nuclear guarantee to Europe. The loss of nuclear superiority, sharpened by the expected vulnerability of American ICBMs, makes it less likely that the United States will respond to a Soviet attack on Europe with a nuclear retaliation on the USSR. This is, of course, an old fear voiced by de Gaulle, among others. But it has grown more acute in recent years, as much in the United States as in Europe. (Indeed, perhaps more so within the United States as the issue became part of the SALT debate).

As others see it, however, the essence of deterrence is still to maintain uncertainty in the mind of the likely aggressor regarding the consequences of his action. No Soviet leader, either massively or in a selective manner, can have confidence that the United States will not punish an attack on Europe. From this perspective, the end of U.S. nuclear superiority has not undermined the American security guarantee.

At the theater nuclear level, the Soviet deployments, if not countered, are seen by some as creating a dangerous gap in NATO's strategy. The improved accuracy and reduced yield of the SS–20s would give the Soviet Union added flexibility against counterforce targets. Faced with the failure of their conventional defense, the allies would resort to battlefield-nuclear weapons, but should Moscow then escalate to the use of the SS–20, it would destroy NATO nuclear-capable aircraft that could be used to strike Soviet territory. This would give the Soviets escalation dominance and leave the United States with the decision of using its central-strategic systems or doing nothing at all. The purpose of deploying new long-range TNFs, therefore, is to fill this new and dangerous gap in NATO's established strategy of flexible response.

Others, however, have pointed out that Western Europe's vulnerability to Soviet IRBMs has existed for more than twenty years and that added selectivity of targeting for the Soviet Union does not represent a significant change for the densely populated societies. Furthermore, the new NATO TNF deployments, by vastly augmenting the ability to strike into Soviet territory from Western Europe, would increase the risk that a nuclear war would be limited to the European continent, thus allowing the United States to remain apart. Accordingly, the argument runs, INF modernization would actually reduce the coupling of U.S. strategic forces with Europe's defense.

This abbreviated discussion of strategic rationales is meant to underscore the ambiguity and inconclusiveness of the military arguments for and against NATO's LRTNF-modernization program. With the doctrinal issues remaining unclear and not providing a sound base for justifying the decisions of government, it is the political factors that have become paramount.

This was already the case in December 1979. The central consideration at that time was what was seen as the political need to respond to the Soviet SS–20 and Backfire deployments. The consensus was that the Western governments could not afford to be seen as doing nothing, either by their own publics or by the USSR. Yet the NATO response was in no way foreordained. Chancellor Schmidt's widely noted comments before the International Institute for Strategic Studies in 1977 about the need to pay attention to the

European nuclear balance was essentially motivated by concerns about preserving European interests in the ongoing SALT II negotiations. The Carter administration in 1978 remained lukewarm to INF modernization, fearing that the issue would detract from its SALT II priorities. (More precisely, the State Department and the White House took this position while the Defense Department talked with Europeans about the virtues of land-based cruise missiles, then in search of a mission.) By the spring of 1979, however, with the growing U.S. debate about the shifting strategic balance and the alleged defense weakness of the Carter administration, the United States swung firmly behind the INF-modernization proposal. A concrete alliance response to Soviet modernization was portrayed as a political imperative, lest there be an impression created of a deteriorated Western will. In the wake of the neutron-bomb fiasco, moreover, it was essential that this decision be a symbol of alliance cohesion. By this time the Europeans had also made clear that they did not want to be deprived of cruise-missile technology in some form or other.

Yet gnawing doubts about the wisdom of the NATO action were already to be found in a number of European countries. It was these reservations, more than the opportunity for arms control, that led to the second track of simultaneously seeking negotiations with the USSR.

Today, more than two years later, the military ambiguities have become still more complicated by the nonratification of SALT II. The coming into force of the treaty had been taken as a given, and it was assumed that arms control negotiations on nuclear weapons in Europe would be folded into SALT III before the expiration of the SALT II protocol in December, 1981. The political uncertainties have been greatly magnified by several factors involving the overall deterioration of East-West relations, differing perceptions as to how to deal with the USSR, and the interplay of foreign policy and domestic politics in a number of countries. Thus, there is now a real possibility that the December 1979 decision of NATO could unravel with serious consequences for the Alliance and for European-American relations.

In a rather fundamental manner, the dominant political perspectives and societal moods have diverged on the two sides of the Atlantic. Troubled by Afghanistan, Poland, the increase in Soviet-American tensions, and the more unstable international-political environment, the Europeans emphasize the importance of maintaining the dialogue with the Soviet Union as a way of constraining its behavior. They are skeptical about the benefits of confronting Moscow, and especially about the tendency of the Reagan administration to see instability in the Third World primarily in East-West terms. The American administration, deeply concerned about the Soviet military buildup at all levels and a pattern of Soviet expansionism in Afghanistan, Africa, the Caribbean, and Central America, places its emphasis on strengthening the military power of the United States and NATO as the best means of affecting

Soviet behavior. It is skeptical about the value of détente, concerned about the growth of pacifism and neutralism in Western Europe, and irritated with what it sees as European military weakness and political softness.

Not surprisingly, the divergence in perspectives comes out most starkly on the issue of arms control. At least until early 1982, the Reagan administration tended to downplay the role that arms control should have in national-security policy and explicitly rejected making weapons-acquisition programs dependent on arms control considerations. It stressed the importance of negotiating from a position of military strength and sought to link progress in arms control with Soviet behavior worldwide. The Europeans, on the other hand, have a stronger interest in arms control now than ever before. Feeling highly vulnerable and geographically exposed, they view arms control as a way of increasing stability on the Continent and restraining Soviet impulses. The greater the danger of war, the more the need for entering into negotiations to limit weapons. Not inclined to follow the Reagan administration's lead in augmenting the defense budget, they also see arms control as a way of avoiding additional military spending and programs. Some Europeans have consistently viewed TNF arms control as a way of making TNF modernization unnecessary.

Support for the NATO TNF-modernization plan exists but is noteworthy for its limits. The opposition is particularly strong in Northern Europe, while in Italy it remains relatively weak, and in France (a nonparticipant) it hardly exists. It is growing, fanned in no small way the the badly timed and insensitive manner with which Washington announced the decision to produce the neutron bomb. No simple characterization of the opposition can be adequate, for it consists of many diverse groups of varied interests and preferences. These encompass a broad antinuclear group that includes, not only those opposed to nuclear weapons, but also many who resist nuclear power, environmentalists, church leaders and religious organizations, pacifists, "Ban the Bomb" protestors, and many others on the traditional left. No doubt the USSR is active in seeking to manipulate public opinion against the NATO program; it is waging a propoganda war with the United States for European sympathies. Anti-Americanism has also increased during the past year, in large part as a reaction to some of the early rhetoric of the Reagan administration.

It would be a mistake, however, to think of all of the opposition as extremist or marginal in either intellectual or political terms. Intellectually, opposition or serious reservations are to be found among many customary supporters of NATO and the Western-security system. Politically, the opposition is becoming more organized, and reservations are held by important political groupings in most of the countries that are due to accept deployment of the missile systems.

The key country is West Germany, which took the lead within Europe in promoting TNF modernization and which insisted upon the nonsingularity

Long-Range-Theater Nuclear Forces

Figure 4–1. A–7 Aircraft

principle, whereby other nations would also need to accept the basing of the cruise missile. German officials were very active in persuading their European colleagues of the necessity for the NATO decision and they accepted for their country the largest portion of the new system (all the 108 Pershing IIs and 96 of the cruise missiles). Should Germany back out, the entire NATO program would surely collapse immediately. The Federal Republic is in an especially delicate situation, not only because of its geographic location and its special stakes in detente arising out of the division of the German people, but also because it is the only one of the three principle European nations to be nonnuclear. Opposition to the TNF plan is considerable and even threatens to undermine the Schmidt government. Although public-opinion polls indicate that a narrow majority of West Germans accept the need for the new missiles, a substantial part of the governing Social Democratic Party, as well as its coalition partner, the Free Democratic Party, does not. The opponents aim to push through a resolution against the TNF modernization at the SPD party conference in 1983. Chancellor Schmidt has threatened to resign if he loses the support of the party on this issue.

The strongest opposition is to be found in the Netherlands which is scheduled to base forty-eight cruise missiles. By one estimate there are 400 different peace groups fighting them in this small country, and the issue long paralyzed the nation, with the Christian Democrats, who support the NATO program, unable to form a governing coalition. Dutch participation has always been highly uncertain, however, and if it were the only dropout this would not be fatal. Belgium is more critical, however, and is likely to be influenced by the ultimate outcome in the Netherlands. It has yet to commit itself unequivocally to basing forty-eight missiles on its soil. As in the case of West Germany, support for the deployments would be better augmented by signs that arms control negotiations are progressing. In Britain, the Thatcher government has been firmly committed to basing 160 cruise missiles, but the Labour Party, while divided on LRTNF, has adopted a platform opposing all nuclear deployments in the United Kingdom. Here the issue has become entangled with the debate on the future of Britain's nuclear deterrent and the Conservative decision to continue it with the purchase of the Trident I. Should the Labour Party come into power, the basing of the cruise missiles could be stopped, especially if the government were headed by Michael Foot. The unilateral-nuclear-disarmament movement is now being revived with vigor and is being spread across the channel by Professor E.P. Thompson with his European Nuclear Disarmament campaign. Among the countries scheduled to base the LRTNFs, only in Italy does dissent remain fairly limited. Thus far the Communists have chosen to stress their national identity and their independence from Moscow by supporting the NATO program. They wish to appear responsible and capable of governing. A switch in political tactics resulting from extraneous considerations could, however, quickly and dramatically alter the outlook.

The arguments of the critics of LRTNF modernization are almost as varied as the opponents are heterogenous. They can be reduced, however, to several key debates:

1. The new weapons would increase the risk of war in Europe. They would create an escalation in the arms race.
2. The substantial increase in longer-range weapons would make it more likely that the two superpowers would feel capable of waging "limited" nuclear war in Europe while avoiding a two-way strategic-nuclear exchange between themselves. The United States is conjuring warfighting scenarios centered upon Europe that would leave it itself immune and, in effect, isolated from the conflict.
3. Neither the existence of nuclear parity between the superpowers nor the deployment of SS–20s and Backfire bombers fundamentally alters the U.S. security guarantee or creates any important new military advantages for the Soviet Union over NATO.
4. Others, who accept the view that the Soviet-force expansion should not go unchallenged by the West, nevertheless feel that priority should be given to arms control negotiations with the USSR without simultaneous NATO deployments that could prejudice the talks.
5. The Reagan administration is not serious about arms control. The U.S. proposal of a zero option is not serious, as it is unlikely to lead to productive results. The administration really seeks to regain American nuclear superiority.
6. Washington is embarked upon a confrontation with Moscow and the LRTNF deployments would drag Europe into it on an issue on which the USSR is ultrasensitive. Instead attention should be focused on maintaining detente.

There are counterarguments to each of these points heard in Europe and many of them contain much validity and persuasiveness. Deployment of the new LRTNF would actually have the effect of recoupling the U.S. deterrent. It would shore up the credibility of the nuclear guarantee, since Moscow would not draw a distinction between an American warhead coming from Europe and one coming from the United States or from the sea. To give arms control negotiations priority over modernization would undermine the Western negotiating position, especially given that the USSR has built a massive lead with its own INF deployments of recent years. The USSR now has approximately 300 of the SS–20s in place, approximately two-thirds of them are targeted on Western Europe, with NATO having almost nothing comparable. The USSR can hardly be expected to dismantle these new weapons if the West does not have something equivalent to bargain with.

Such responses to the dissenters have not been given with adequate clarity and conviction by European leaders of govenment. In turn, European leaders have not been assisted by some of the criticisms that have been made by leading Americans regarding the attitudes of the allies. To accuse the Europeans of adopting a philosophy of better-red-than-dead or to say that the opponents of the neutron bomb are really carrying the propoganda ball for the USSR is not conducive to mutual understanding. It betrays considerable annoyance and impatience with the Euorpean allies. It results in a growing unease about American assertiveness and domination, and a loss of confidence in U.S. wisdom and its capacity for leading the West.

The final outcome of the debate within Europe is not possible to predict. One of its disturbing aspects is that it could go on throughout the decade of the eighties. The last LRTNF placements now planned are not due until 1988 and it would be a miracle if they were not victim to some of the same delays that almost all weapons programs suffer. Meanwhile, the missiles will be subject to the pushes and strains of domestic politics. Governments in the basing countries, many of which are dependent on fragile coalitions, will be vulnerable to political attacks using the nuclear missiles as an issue. Moreover, the LRTNF deployments could also become hostage to the condition of the broader European-American political relationship. Clashes between Europeans and the United States on such issues as internal change in Central America or policy toward the Middle East, if sufficiently heated and deep, could well spill over and affect attitudes toward the defense of Europe. Anti-Americanism can have many sources and varied results. The protest movement against new nuclear weapons in Europe has no doubt been augmented by disagreements with U.S. policy in El Salvador.

For the moment the NATO-modernization plan remains, more or less, on track. A final commitment has not been made by Belgium, and The Netherlands should probably not be counted on, but West Germany, Britain, and Italy remain committed. The entire situation, however, is highly precarious and the longer-term outlook cannot be comforting. Responsible thought must urgently be given to what can be done to either build up support for the current NATO plan or to present an alternative capable of achieving wider acceptance.

To allow the December 1979 commitments simply to unravel would, in my judgment, be politically disastrous. The consequences for the cohesion and integrity of the Atlantic Alliance could be very great indeed. The NATO-modernization plan was undertaken by the Alliance as a whole after months of planning and deliberation. A total collapse would lead to a long period of political acrimony. It would cast grave doubt on the ability of NATO to deal with any new nuclear-weapons program in the future. It would substantially undermine support in the United States for its commitment to NATO and for the defense of Europe. It would also send precisely the wrong signals to the USSR: that it can engage in its own force modernization without a Western response, that there clearly has occurred a serious erosion of Western will and resolve, and perhaps even that the USSR can now indirectly interfere with NATO's defense strategy. Without an acceptable alternative, the resulting crisis in confidence would be severe. The damage to NATO could be substantial and lasting.

A two-step approach might now be undertaken. The first step would be to reduce the opposition to the LRTNF plan by making concrete progress in arms control. The second would be for NATO to consider seriously what might be a more acceptable mix of long-range weapons and basing modes in the form of sea-based systems.

Clearly, progress in arms control for nuclear forces in Europe would defuse a major part of the current opposition. Support for the second, arms control, track of December 1979 decision has consistently been strong in Europe. The opening of the Geneva negotiations with the Soviet Union was an overdue step in the right direction. It is important, however, that there be no illusions. It is highly improbable that an arms-control agreement can be reached along the lines of the zero option that President Reagan has proposed. Some level of LRTNF deployments will be necessary, unless the Soviet Union agrees to dismantle all or close to all of its SS–20s. It would be unrealistic to expect Soviet agreement to take such a step. For the Americans, it is important that they not be under the illusion that procedural or inconclusive talks can be used as a placebo to pacify the Europeans indefinitely. The Europeans have in the past decade become far more sophisticated and knowledgeable observers of, and in some areas participants in, East-West arms control. Identifiable results, or, at a minimum, the conviction that Washington is making a strong and sincere attempt to make progress in negotiations with Moscow, will be required.

Options for nuclear arms control in Europe are outside the scope of this chapter. It is perfectly evident, however, that the negotiations will be extremely complex. The USSR will start with a very substantial advantage making the creation of a regional balance, or parity, difficult to achieve. But, in addition, there is no accepted understanding about which systems are to be included in the negotiations or even what the Western objectives should be. Such issues, moreover, cannot be adequately addressed without an overarching policy for arms control involving the central-strategic systems of the superpowers. A return to the SALT/START process is therefore essential to INF arms control.

Because the outlook for early and successful progress in limiting nuclear arms in Europe is bleak (and bearing in mind the necessity for establishing adequate political support in Europe for any nuclear-modernization program) NATO, at an appropriate time, might reexamine a sea-based system as an alternative to the present plans. This need not be perceived as a political retreat; rather, it would be comparable to the reappraisal of MX alternatives under way in the United States. Indeed, should the MX be replaced by a new sea-based missile, as advocated by some, a parallel move in Europe might instantly muster considerable interest.

From a military perspective, sea basing would have significant benefits. Cruise missiles or ballistic missiles at sea would have excellent mobility, concealability, and therefore invulnerability—unlike the GLCMs and Pershing IIs whose survivability will depend upon covertness and operational skill in scrambling during a crisis. Command and control might be a problem, but cruise missiles at sea should be just as accurate as their land-based brethren. Placing LRTNF at sea would have the added advantage of reducing the targets available in Western Europe for the Soviet Union's nuclear forces.

Why, then, did NATO favor the land-based systems in 1979? There were two sets of reasons. The cost of sea-based system, whether on new or converted submarines, or on fast surface craft, would have been higher, and the naval systems would not have been available until later in the decade. The preference of the Pentagon was for land-based systems because of its own program priorities. The second, and for this discussion more consequential reason, was that land-based systems provided greater visibility for the European publics. This could be more widely seen as a physical link between European soil and the U.S. strategic deterrent.

These considerations should be reappraised under the present circumstances. From the viewpoint of visibility, having the missiles out at sea might now be a bonus. The predicted public marches on the GLCM and Pershing II locations could be forgotten. There is still much appeal in the jingle of two decades ago about the MLF: "Put the missile out to sea/Where the real estate is free/And it's far away from me. . . ."

As for the political/psychological argument for the visibility of the coupling weapons, if the Europeans themselves are satisfied with weapons at sea—as some opponents of current plans have indicated they would be—there is no reason why this should be discouraged by the United States. After all, it is the Europeans who are meant to be reassured by the new systems. As to the cost and time factors, surely these should not be overriding concerns on an issue as sensitive and important as this. In sum, if in moving the LRTNF to sea much of the opposition to the current NATO plan would disappear and a far wider base of domestic support could be found, then such an alternative becomes very attractive.

The political dimension is the critical element. We are dealing with problems of credibility regarding the USSR, and confidence within the Atlantic Alliance. Nuclear weapons are the currency but their primary role (let us hope) is to serve as political symbols. For the past quarter-century the nuclear arrangements within the Atlantic Alliance have been highly sensitive and the subject of recurring controversy. This will continue for as long as Western Europe remains dependent on American deterrence capabilities. The task will be to manage the issue, for there is no solution at hand. In this task, the next several years may well be the most challenging yet.

Long-Range-Theater Nuclear Forces 49

Figure 4-2. FB-111A Aircraft Launching a Short-Range Attack Missile

# Security Policy and Arms Control: A European Perspective

Klaas G. de Vries

Background: A Fragmented Consensus

Security issues—in particular the role of negotiations in security policy—are currently the source of increasing tension in the transatlantic relationship. Such issues are especially serious since they affect the fundamental justification for the Atlantic Alliance. Yet it is important to remember that the disagreement over security policy and arms control is as much a product of intra-alliance tensions as it is a cause of them. In many ways it symbolizes the fragmentation of the larger economic, security, and foreign-policy consensus that has underpinned the alliance.

In the security area, the growing differences in perspective on both sides of the Alliance are of a more serious nature than the familiar claim that the Alliance is in disarray. In alliance countries on both sides of the Atlantic, public interest in security has increased substantially. But the commonality of interest has not been matched by a commonality of response. Public opinion has marched in very different directions. In the United States, a forceful and well-organized campaign has been waged to provide for radical changes in the country's security policy. From the time President Reagan took office an unprecedented expansion of armaments was initiated with, it appears, the almost overwhelming support of Congress. Thus the American public appears to support the administration's contention that greater military power will provide the key to the challenges of the 1980s. By contrast, the increased awareness in Europe has produced a questioning of current defense policies and particularly the role of nuclear weapons. Peace movements, church groups, and labor unions are questioning the assumptions underlying our security policy and arguing the need for restraint rather than expansion.

In foreign policy, more generally, Europeans feel that military power has proved to be a blunt instrument with which to shape international relations. The increase in the destructive potential of the superpowers has paradoxically led to a relative decline in the scope of its use. Neither superpower has found its possession of nuclear weapons to be an exploitable asset. Other factors have contributed far more to changes in influence than military force. On the one hand, one can point to the redistribution of financial and economic power in the world, exemplified by countries such as Japan, Korea, and the Arabian Gulf states. On the other hand, one can witness the dramatized force of nationalism and religion in former military, politically or culturally suppressed or colonized countries, and the continuing struggle of peoples to rid themselves of self-appointed exploiters.

Europeans tend to recognize the growing complexity of international relations, while the tendency of the present American administration has been to return to rather more simple perspectives of the world. These derive from the belief that only one fundamental distinction in the world colors all international relations: the ideological differences between the Western world and the Communist world. A telling example of this school of thought was presented during the visit of the Secretary of State, Alexander Haig, to the Middle East in 1981 when he wished to establish a strategic consensus. A simple choice by the countries in the region between Washington and Moscow, however, did not appeal to the strategic instincts of Israelis or Arabs, let alone the Palestinians. More shocking is the use of this either/or approach in United States policies toward Central America. One could argue of course that nothing better could be expected, given the inability of Washington (for more than twenty years) to normalize its relationship with Cuba. Nevertheless the distinction made in Washington today between authoritarian and totalitarian regimes is not only appalling for its intellectual inconsistencies, but, above all, in the light of the abhorrent policies that it seeks to condone.

The different views on so many issues reflect the contrasting evolution of the two Atlantic communities. American and European societies have been subject to different influences and pressures. Initially preoccupied with economic recovery, European attention has been focused on the slow and somewhat tortuous path to economic and political integration. Within the community, Britain and France have adapted to a more modest role, while the Federal Republic has played an increasingly important role especially with regard to Eastern Europe. Economically, Europe has developed into one of the world's most important markets and in this area has become the equal of the United States. But the lessons of postwar European development have been those of patience, moderation, perseverence, and above all, continuity. Changes in leadership have brought differences of style, but the political line has remained remarkably consistent.

The changes that the United States has experienced have been somewhat more dramatic. The United States emerged from World War II as the natural leader of the Western world. The unique combination of a victorious war record, overwhelming military strength, an impressive comparative economic affluence, and an enormously attractive openness and directness of its society made the United States NATO's natural leader. Its main concern was to manage the recurring problem of being a credible lion without scaring the ladies. Much of this has now disappeared. The military power of the United States has for all practical purposes been equally by the Soviet Union. The United States was humiliated in a highly controversial war in Vietnam. Its economic strength has practically been matched by Europe and Japan. Over the last decade, American society has experienced an unfamiliar sense of vulnerability in economic, military, and political terms.

The apparent incapacity to deal with these pressures has produced a lack of faith in American leadership. Since the demise of the Carter administration—appreciated for its intentions and criticized for its weak hand—the Reagan administration has appeared with its reassuringly simplistic view of the world. But the abrupt changes in foreign policy have been met elsewhere with skepticism. Washington's rigorous, almost confrontational, attitude toward the USSR is considered both dangerous and counterproductive by many Europeans. Europe resists American pressure to view the world through East-West filters. Thus the present transatlantic dialogue starts sounding like the exchange between the Lone Ranger and Tonto:

"Tonto, we're in big trouble."
"What do you mean 'we' Kemosabi?"

The Alliance: Defining Security

In discussing the current conflict in the Alliance over security and arms control, it is worthwhile remembering the analysis and recommendations of the so-called Harmel Report, on which the fifteen governments of NATO agreed in 1967. As the Report notes, the alliance has two functions: "Its first function is to maintain adequate military strength and political solidarity to deter aggression and other forms of pressure and to defend the territory of the member countries if aggression should occur." The second function of the Alliance is

> to pursue the search for progress towards a more stable relationship in which the underlying issues can be solved. Military security and a policy of detente are not contradictory but complementary. Collective defense is a stabilizing factor in world politics. It is the necessary condition for effective policies directed towards a greater relaxation of tensions. The way to peace and stability in Europe rests in particular on the use of the Alliance constructively in the interest of detente.

Further on, the report reads:

Each Ally should play its full part in promoting an improvement in relations with the Soviet Union and the countries of Eastern Europe, bearing in mind that the pursuit of detente must not be allowed to split the Alliance. The changes of success will clearly be greater if the Allies remain on parallel courses, especially in matters of close concern to them all; their actions will thus be all the more effective.[1]

Today, there is considerable doubt whether all Allies still subscribe to the thrust of the Harmel Report. Is the ultimate goal of the Alliance still "to achieve a just and lasting peaceful order in Europe, accompanied by appropriate security guarantees?" Succeeding American administrations have had difficulties in understanding and appreciating the inseparable combination of military security and a policy of detente, which is at the heart of European security policies. Gerald Ford scrapped the word detente from the political dictionary of the Alliance and replaced it by the formula of peace through strength. The present American administration has reluctantly agreed to detente if "genuine." But it is known to feel that an excessive preoccupation with detente has virtually aborted the results of many years of negotiations on the limitation of nuclear weapons and sees the expansion of Soviet power as the most urgent issue of foreign policy.

Secretary Haig stated that reciprocity and strength would be more appropriate guidelines than detente to deal with the challenges of the 1980's. According to Eugene Rostow, Director of the Arms Control and Disarmament Agency, the United States and its allies should return to the policy of containment which, it is argued, will require a substantial buildup of American and West European military strength.

Many Europeans regard the American preoccupation with an ever-growing and all-consuming Soviet threat as an unbalanced approach to security.[2] Europeans continue to devote considerable sums to defense, but popular support for current defense policies is dependent on retaining the dual emphasis of NATO's defense and detente policies. Public opinion will not support a reliance solely on military buildup. The concept of detente and the gradual expansion of relations with the East must continue alongside the implementation of defense policies.

It is not difficult to see why Europeans persist in stressing that normalization must be an equal component of Western security policy. The reasons have little to do with fear of the USSR or loss of faith in the United States. They are based on the very simple and practical belief that long-term security rests in the construction of a political and economic framework between East and West.

The quite natural fear of being a potential battlefield ranks high in the public perception and guides reaction to policies that appear to concentrate exclusively on the development of military capabilities. War can be avoided through the retention of credible military strength, but lasting political stability can be assured only through the creation of a political structure that encourages mutual interdependence and dissipates mutual suspicion.

In Europe, adherence to the philosophy of the Harmel Report is considered of vital importance for preserving peace. Many Europeans are deeply worried about the dramatic shift of emphasis in American policy on defense spending, while American professions of sincerity for arms control appear hollow and disingenuous. Indeed, it is the American shift on arms control that has been responsible for so much of the public agitation in Europe. Arms-control negotiations, and particularly the SALT process, have come to symbolize the desire and the commitment of the two superpowers to seek agreement on the most crucial part of their relationship. The common responsibility for the continuation of this process remains, no matter what changes occur in more peripheral areas of the relationship.

The Alliance: Arms Control in Defense Policy

It cannot be denied that contemporary arms control has been a precarious process. As Senator Joseph R. Biden has observed:

> Arms control has fallen under simultaneous seige by two rival armies, each equipped with a formidable critique. One has attacked from the right, the other stands to the left. Together, each led by articulate proponents, they seem ready to overwhelm those still holding out in defense of patient efforts toward formal arms limitation.[3]

Burdened with unduly optimistic objectives, mixed with spasms of pragmatic and sometimes cynical appraisals of its limitations, the process sometimes has led to great public frustration. The urge for symmetrical reductions, the neglect of qualitative changes, the extreme preoccupation with verification problems, and the unavoidable inclination to out-fox the adversary with bargaining chips are not precisely ingredients for dramatic results. But despite these shortcomings, arms control negotiations have a crucial role in the East-West dialogue. It has made eminent sense to talk to the adversary about our respective military capabilities and to attempt to establish mutually acceptable limitations. Negotiations, therefore, are essential to the long-term objective of stability and better mutual confidence in the West's relations with the USSR. For this reason, they find a strong constituency in Europe.

Arms control policies can only promote alliance cohesion and be a means to pursue stability and predictability if conducted in a reliable and consistent manner. Unfortunately, the history of United States arms control policies so far has been full of surprises, particularly in the last two years.

For example, the leaders and officials of four successive American administrations confirmed that SALT II was in the interests of the Alliance. After the SALT II Treaty was signed by the American president and the president of the Soviet Union, the new American administration conveyed to the world the news that the SALT II Treaty was fatally flawed. Even worse, it alleged that the arms control process had undermined Western security by distracting members of the Alliance from the steadily growing menace that confronted them. The most poisonous venom of this message was that previous

American administrations were misleading their Allies and negotiating partners, and that the United States at the negotiating table was not to be taken seriously.

The about-turn of the United States is inconsistent with the nature of the Alliance. An alliance of fifteen members cannot suddenly change course on the whim of a single member, even if it is the largest and most capable.

These swings in U.S. arms control policy, the differing Alliance attitudes toward detente, combined with other sources of tension within the Alliance make it important, therefore, to reassess and think through some of the general principles that should guide our future security policy. The first priority is that a credible defense policy and a credible arms control policy should contribute to the enhancement of security in a mutually supportive way. Without self-restraint in defense policies, negotiated constraints will be sought in vain. The pursuit of military superiority through the buildup of armaments and the pursuit of parity and equivalence in arms control is self-contradictory. Weapon decisions cannot responsibly be taken before the implications for arms control have been thoroughly discussed. This implies, of course, that the initial approach of the Reagan administration in 1981, promoting a huge increase in defense spending before setting even the contours of an arms control policy, was a fundamental mistake.

NATO's Strategy

In essence, NATO's strategy of deterrence is based on the perception of the risks a potential adversary might be prepared to take. Inevitably, this involves calculation of his capabilities. But the adversary's capabilities should only comprise one element of the security equation. It is important to recognize that the armed forces of the two alliances evolve from very different historical, social, and political circumstances and serve very different strategic needs. Furthermore, there are a range of qualitative and quantitative factors that are extremely difficult to assess. Thus, comparison of numbers—on which so many security assessments are based—is not meaningful. Because of the inherent difficulties of measurement and comparison, there may be no better solution than to accept a notional balance of forces—one that is consistent with NATO's broader political objectives for stability, but equally appropriate to its perceived requirements for security and its capacity and willingness to meet the associated expenditures.

Furthermore, the Alliance will never develop a defense posture that so convincingly guarantees its security that the Warsaw Pact's perceptions and concerns can be dismissed. In fact, it should be recognized that such a goal is contrary to the very nature of the Alliance and is in any case politically misguided. In the nuclear age, there can be no such goal as superiority or total security. Improvements to military capabilities are obviously necessary to ensure the credibility of deterrence but military capabilities alone do not provide the basis for lasting security; in the absence of a political framework, they serve primarily to heighten the anxieties and suspicions of the other side. Arms control policy, on the other hand, can provide that element of assurance and predictability and can ensure that modernization is restrained. Defense without detente is security without foundation.

Of course, this process is continually under challenge from those who seek the unobtainable goal of infinite security, or who insist on basing their assessments on worst-case scenarios. There has always been a surplus of critics to preach the Alliance's weaknesses. The effect of this criticism has been to weaken self-confidence, to create doubts in the minds of friends and neutrals, and to suggest to Soviet leaders possibilities that do not actually exist. Thus, the final result of their arguments has been to undermine deterrence.

The question of the American nuclear guarantee to Europe is fundamental to the very existence of NATO. During the last two decades, the alliance has sought to prove that the United States would be willing and capable of using its nuclear forces to defend Europe. Despite a variety of measures, of which INF modernization is the latest, the doubts continue to linger. NATO's strategy of deterrence through flexible response and its reliance on nuclear weapons based in Europe is now seriously at issue.

Yet the debate indicates the irony of NATO's deterrent strategies. While the experts worry that the United States would not use their nuclear systems to defend Europe, public concern is precisely that they will. The debate is inevitably confused because it is never clear whether the object is to convince the Soviet Union or to reassure ourselves. In the logic of deterrence theory, the more usable the weapons, the more the enemy is deterred. But in the logic of real life, it is this very usability that public opinion finds most threatening. The search for credible deterrence through making nuclear weapons more usable has raised—more than diminished —international uncertainty and unease, increasingly so as it is seen to be unaccompanied by a coherent and potentially moderating arms control policy.

There is no definitive way to finally reassure those who doubt the efficacy of the American guarantee. The Alice-in-Wonderland nature of the issue was vividly demonstrated by Henry Kissinger, when, in his speech in Brussels on September 1, 1979, he stated that any American secretary of state in the past or future who assured Europeans that American central systems were available for the defense of Europe was not to be believed. The statement issued by Secretary of State Cyrus Vance a few days later, saying that there should be no doubt about the commitment of American nuclear forces in the defense of Europe, left many Europeans puzzled, as did the legendary man from Crete when he informed his audience that all Cretans were liars.

NATO sought refuge from the perplexing and insoluble problem of ensuring credible defense under the mantle of the doctrine of flexible response. The adoption of this strategy earned the Alliance a respite in the form of the relatively passive and noncontroversial 1970s. But it did not solve the contradictions of NATO policy. Moreover, for Europeans—given the destructiveness of nuclear weapons—flexible response in many respects is massive retaliation in another guise. In this sense, the adoption of flexible response merely postponed the basic issues facing NATO and these have now reappeared with renewed force.

Flexible response means the ability to answer aggression at whatever level it is posed. It is essentially an all-things-to-all-men strategy, and, as such, it is open to a broad range of interpretations. Thus, it has to cope with every conceivable threat that a fertile imagination can conceive of. In its extreme form, this strategy can be described as a recipe for an arms race since it provides the justification for the introduction of weapons at every level of escalation. This was acceptable all the time that defense remained the preserve of the bureaucrats and was based on relatively sound economies. However, that time is passed and public opinion is now alive to the contradictions inherent in NATO's present strategy.

The Need for Reappraisal

Two elements in NATO's strategy must be addressed immediately because they are the most urgent aspects of the problems facing the Alliance in establishing its security policy—the question of battlefield nuclear weapons and of LRTNF modernization.

No issue demonstrates the confusion and contradiction in NATO strategy more than the presence of battlefield nuclear weapons in Europe. Their deployment has always raised important issues concerning NATO's nuclear policy but has consistently failed to provide answers. (These problems appear to apply to battlefield-nuclear systems in general and are to come extent reflected in the deployment of similar Soviet weapons). Being at the lowest rung on the ladder of escalation, battlefield weapons—it is sometimes argued—are designed to deter battlefield-nuclear use by an adversary. However, the deployment and operational constraints of these weapons are such that their maximum utility is at an earlier, rather than later, stage of a major conflict.

If the alliance is to seriously address problems of escalation control and the maintenance of credible deterrence, it is appropriate to ask whether these battlefield-nuclear systems could be replaced by advanced-conventional weapons. The technological developments in conventional systems as represented by Assault Breaker, Pershing IIA armed with a precision-guided conventional high-explosive warhead and similarly conventionally armed cruise missiles, would permit NATO to threaten comparable Warsaw Pact targets much as it does now with existing battlefield-nuclear weapons. In addition to threatening the destruction of these target sets, the new conventional systems would be inherently more responsive and, by their deployment pattern, less vulnerable to preemptive attack. This last problem is one to which battlefield nuclear weapons—by virtue of their peacetime security, deployment, and operational-use problems—are especially susceptible.

The Alliance needs to decide whether it can unilaterally withdraw weapon systems whose deployment appears not best-suited to its security. (This is especially so when alternative and superior solutions are at hand.) NATO should consider withdrawing all battlefield-nuclear systems and all nuclear warheads associated with battlefield systems. Besides being in NATO's interest, this move would also constitute an important political gesture toward reassuring the public over Alliance nuclear policies. If NATO continues to maintain battlefield nuclear weapons simply because the Soviet Union has them, it hands over the initiative for its force planning to its adversary.[4]

As if the problems generated by battlefield-nuclear systems did not present NATO with enough difficulties, the issue of INF has been added to the agenda. Questions relating to the need for INF from a military and political perspective are still the subject of intense debate.[5] The history of the December 1979 decision seems to suggest a serious discrepancy between the political and military rationales. The NATO dual-track decision is a classical "fudge," it accommodates both the modernizers and the arms controllers, but leaves the general public throughly confused as to what this exercise is meant to achieve. Are the deployments to correct deficiences in NATO's strategy of flexible response, or are they to counter Soviet deployments? Are new systems necessary in view of the thousands of strategic warheads already stockpiled? What do Eurostrategic balances really matter in the alliance? What wisdom is there in rigid adherence to the selected deployment mode of the systems on land, instead of at sea? Why have many of the arguments in favor of modernization linked this program directly to the Russian SS-20?

Among the political arguments, visibility—notably for Western Europeans—has ranked very high, and has often been related to the question of coupling. Supporters argue that deployment of the new systems would demonstrate to the Europeans that the United States would be more likely to use its nuclear force against an agressor. Others have argued that the Russians being fired at with American nuclear weapons would immediately involve American territory in a nuclear exchange. Thus an unreliable ally would be forced to assist Europe by a—solely for this purpose—reliable enemy. (Of course, a skeptic might conclude that the United States could hope over time to accustom the USSR to the fact that if the worst came to worst, a limited nuclear exchange would be preferable to all-out nuclear war—except for the Europeans.) Coupling, however, will never mechanistically result from the deployment mode or type of nuclear weapons. Whether or not faith can be placed in the American nuclear commitment to Europe will therefore continue to be an interesting topic for debate.

The NATO decision of December 1979 to introduce new nuclear systems in Europe attributed an essential role to arms control. Two years later, preparations for production and deployment of the new missiles were well under way. For negotiations, two years were lost. The negotiations on INF in Geneva, having commenced belatedly at the end of 1981, have no chance of succeeding if the rationale for the double-track decision of 1979 is not reassessed and clarified. It is essential to establish whether the Pershing II and GLCM are needed, or whether they are only designed to obtain a balance with the USSR in the totally artificial and compartmentalized area of Eurostrategic systems. If the latter, then what are the precise objectives—how many SS-20s is NATO prepared to live with and how many INF does the German chancellor need to feel secure? So far, the advocates of balance have provided no clear idea of what the nuclear balance ought to look alike. The question of which systems to include from a negotiating perspective opens a Pandora's box. The original NATO approach of a narrow and selective focus on land-based missiles was produced as the only way considered likely to make progress. Progress, of course, was necessary in order to sustain public support for deployments. Yet concentration on land-based missiles does not address the threat perceptions of either side of the negotiating table. Undoubtably, areas not covered by negotiations will lead to the discovery of new gaps and more double decisions in the future.

The contradictions inherent in the current NATO approach and, indeed, in the double decision, are now painfully obvious. An obsession with a selective and narrow concept of balance led to a situation where, in the modernization program, NATO stressed that it did not aim for numerical parity (just a matching capability), whereas in the arms control package, the Alliance has insisted that the right to numerical parity must be established.

The only realistic solution to the predicament the Alliance finds itself in is to return the question of long-range nuclear systems to the central balance, that is, the SALT process. American systems based in Europe should be considered in the overall context of the strategic forces deployed by either side. This is the situation which would have normally been the case if the SALT II Treaty had been ratified, and the United States and the Soviet Union had moved on to SALT III. This is not to underestimate the complexity of such a negotiating position, but at least it would allow for a logical negotiating framework. The fact that no SALT framework exists is clearly an impediment to this proposal. However, the longer the United States delays developing a SALT position the more reason the European partners have to argue for a review of the current LRTNF decision. The American negotiating position in Geneva is based on a global consideration of intermediate-range systems.

Security Policy and Arms Control

Given the totally different geographical composition of the Warsaw Pact and NATO, one cannot hope for success by concentrating on systems with a certain range without integrating them with talks on so-called strategic systems.

Moreover, it is hard to envisage any results coming from Geneva if another element in the American negotiating posture is not reconsidered. So far, the Reagan administration seeks to compare only American intermediate-range systems with Soviet systems, without giving any consideration to the existence of the nuclear forces of other NATO members, France and the United Kingdom. It seems incomprehensible to read in the communique of the Nuclear Planning Group of NATO, meeting in Colorado Springs in April 1982, that the British deterrent is of fundamental importance to the alliance, while in Geneva the relevance of this force (and of the French nuclear forces) is being denied. This is a recipe for a failure. There is no way in which we could kindly ask the Soviets not to take those nuclear forces into account. Besides having read the NPG communique they will have noticed British advisors in the NATO advisory group for the Geneva talks.

There are other reasons that would justify a call for a reassessment of the NATO decision. Despite what the alliance affirms today, the 1979 decision clearly subordinated the principle of arms control to the principle of modernization. NATO took the need to deploy the new systems as the starting point for its arms control approach. When the Big Four met in Guadaloupe in 1979, they had already agreed on the necessity of modernization, adding the arms control offer to make the decision acceptable to public opinion. Moreover, the December 12 decision was adopted in a very different political environment. European governments backed the decision on the understanding that there was a clear American commitment to arms control (one only has to recollect the last-minute visits of three European leaders to seek President Carter's personal assurances on this issue), but in the Reagan adminstration this commitment has taken a far lower priority. If there had not been the pressure of the European partners, the Geneva talks would never have commenced. The beginning of the talks on strategic systems was delayed because of the application of linkage. Soviet involvement in Poland has been called the major factor for the delay. So while INF talks could proceed despite the Polish crisis and START talks had to be delayed because of the Polish crisis, one had to wonder whether the American government still believed that negotiations on nuclear weapons were meant to do our adversaries a favor.

The strategic context has also changed. The new administration's strategic plans, particularly the deployment at sea of 3,000 or more cruise missiles, means that NATO's 572 missiles will be deployed in a very different strategic environment from that envisaged in 1979.

A proposal to reexamine the NATO decision in order to allow for a thorough reassessment will, of course, be fiercely opposed. The NATO decision has now become less a decision about the deployment of nuclear missiles and more a test of NATO's ability to make decisions, no matter how much they are overtaken by events. However, those who foresee the dire consequences of a reassessment would be well-advised to look at the consequences of trying to force the decision in light of domestic opposition and an inadequate Alliance position on arms control. The long-term damage to European public support for the alliance could be incalculable.

Some will argue that a reassessment of the double decision by NATO will mean that the Soviet expansion of theater forces will go unanswered, but the question of how to respond to developments on the other side can be answered in different ways. The American preference has always been to meet the challenge by a buildup of her own. In Europe, many argue that before weapon decisions are taken, a political attempt must be to made to try to achieve an acceptable result. In 1979, in a report to the North Atlantic Assembly, the author argued:

> In the Rapporteur's view, the arms control option should be pursued before any decision is made concerning the deployment of new capabilities. In his view, the potential options are far enough advanced in their development phase to present a real and credible threat to the Soviet Union. If, as is reported, the Soviet Union has a deep and genuine concern over the potential introduction of cruise missiles into the European theatre, then it must realize that with the ALCM close to deployment (the first ALCM-equipped B-52 squadrons will be deployed in 1981) then the deployment of SLCM's or GLCM's cannot be far behind. The existence and status of these programs, and the capability of the Alliance to implement them if satisfactory results are not obtained through negotiating should be sufficient to obtain satsifactory restraints on Soviet systems.

Of course, this proposal was made when many believed, including the author and his parliamentary colleagues, that the situation remained open and that the Alliance was still attempting to seek a political solution. Now it is known that the issue had already been decided at Guadaloupe where the Big Four had agreed on the principle of modernization. At the same time, they had also agreed that this decision would be made more palatable to public opinion by an offer to commence arms control negotiations. Despite what alliance officials claim today, it is clear that the principle of arms control was always subordinate to the principle of modernization. Indeed, the arms control approach developed by NATO took as its starting point the need to deploy new systems, thus the Special Group was created to legitimize the work of the HLG. Equally regrettable was the fact that a decision of immediate consequence and concern to all members of the Alliance was settled in this arbitrary fashion by the Big Four, one of whom—France—had no immediate involvement with the decision.

Still it seems that double decisions might prove difficult to sustain over an extended period of time. They lack credibility in the eyes of friends and foes alike, and their implementation is easily manipulated to serve the interest of one of the parties involved. Also, the dynamics of a production decision for new weapons obviously have more momentum than those of a decision to negotiate. A basic objection to the approach chosen in 1979, however, seems to be that the Alliance has not managed to remain master of its own decisions. In a sense, the Soviet Union has been invited to the table of the NATO Council in order to help increase the confusion about the security policy of the Alliance. This dilemma could only be solved if the Alliance would be prepared to take a fresh look at the decisions it took in 1979. If the Alliance is not politically capable of doing so, it will have to cope with increasingly fragmentary tensions internally.

Conclusion

Discrepancies within the Alliance are deepening; transatlantic perspectives on security reflect a very different order of priorities. Friction of this nature is traditional, but is now more acute because public opinion is seriously engaged. Support for the Alliance and for defense is being undermined because NATO's current security policy is out of phase with the economic and political environment. Public pressures point to the need for a new approach. It is essential that public opinion be able to identify with the objectives and capabilities of NATO's defense strategy. Security cannot remain the prerogative of specialists whose arcane language has little or no meaning to the general public, except for the prospect of nuclear oblivion.

Europe has traditionally played a subordinate role to the United States in determining Alliance security policy, with European reservations too often swept aside in the interest of that magic formula—Alliance unity. That time has passed. Europeans must now play a more forceful role in determining the future requirements of Western security. They must insist that the Alliance returns to the duality of defense and detente as the basis for Western security. A reassessment would begin with the most pressing issue of the day—the role of nuclear weapons. NATO should withdraw all nuclear warheads associated with battlefield systems. This would provide an important demonstration of the West's commitment to restraint rather than expansion of nuclear weapons. The NATO December 12 decision should be reviewed. Deployment should be postponed in order to allow for the devleopment of an arms control approach that avoids the narrow and illusory focus on land-based systems and places LRTNF within the broader context of SALT.

This development would be entirely dependent on U.S. willingness to moderate its current stance and to demonstrate greater enthusiasm for arms control than is so far apparent. If the United States is unwilling to return to a more balanced approach to security, then the European partners will have little alternative but to exert the only leverage they have—the refusal to permit the deployment of nuclear weapons on European territory. The consequences of this development would be far-reaching, but they must be measured against the consequences of a continuation of current trends. Without the twin pillars of defense and detente, NATO is of questionable value, and it will increasingly be seen to be so by European public opinion. The United States is rapidly isolating itself in many areas of foreign policy, particularly from the Third World. The European partners have a duty to attempt to influence the current administration toward a more constructive and balanced approach to security issues. But if, as is likely, this administration is not listening, then European governments have no option other than to develop and pursue their own approach to the East. A continuation of current United States policies will represent an abdication of leadership of the West, because America will have ceased to represent the wishes of those it professes to lead.

Notes

1. The Future Task of the Alliance; Report of the Council Annex of the Ministerial Meeting, December 1967.
2. An interesting example of the Reagan administration's myopic concern with the Soviet threat is provided by American efforts to prevent Western European states from entering into an agreement with the Soviet Union on the delivery of natural gas. During the Ottawa Summit, President Reagan offered to help Western Europe with nuclear energy, if it would only stop negotiations with the Soviet Union. To many Europeans this effort looks like tilting against windmills. Trade between East and West is seen as an essential element in European security policies. It provides mutual advantage to East and West, improves interdependence and promotes useful contacts, all of which are seen as a positive contribution to stability in Europe.
3. For a thoughtful analysis of present tensions in the alliance and the arms control process, see Senator Biden's contribution "Leading the Allies," *Washington Quarterly,* (Summer 1981).
4. According to alliance defense officials, the Soviet Union does not stockpile nuclear warheads in Eastern Europe.
5. For the author's views see: "The Modernization of NATO's Long-Range Theatre Nuclear Forces," Congressional Research Service, Library of Congress; by Simon Lunn (96th Congress, 2nd Session, December 31, 1980) and General Report on the Security of the Alliance: "The Role of Nuclear Weapons", presented by Klaas G. de Vries, General Rapporteur, North Atlantic Assembly—Ottawa, Canada, October 1979 (96th Congress, 2nd Session, Report of the United States Delegation, February, 1980).

Prospects for Limiting Nuclear Forces in Europe

Jane M.O. Sharp

In the late 1950s and early 1960s, attempts to limit nuclear forces in Europe stemmed mainly from Soviet and East European concerns about successive new NATO deployments, in particular the possibility that West Germany would gain access to an independent nuclear arsenal. These early efforts generally took the form of proposals for nuclear free zones in Europe and were rejected by the NATO powers largely because of West German fears of singular treatment within the Alliance. In the late 1960s, withdrawal from Europe of all American land-based missiles capable of reaching Soviet targets, and negotiation of the Non-Proliferation Treaty (NPT), met some of the Eastern bloc's concerns, but the NPT did not prevent NATO allies from providing bases for American (and British) nuclear weapons. Thus, during the 1970s, the Soviets repeatedly sought to include in the SALT ceilings American nuclear-capable aircraft, forward-based in Europe and elsewhere, that could strike Soviet territory, the so-called FBS. These efforts were resisted by the United States on the grounds that European FBS served a NATO defense mission and could not be negotiated away bilaterally.

At the Mutually Balanced Force Reduction (MBFR) talks in Vienna, the Soviets again tried to limit FBS. This effort also failed in the sense that no legally binding limits were imposed, but NATO was interested in trading its nuclear-warhead superiority against Soviet tank strength, and there has been some denuclearization of dual-capable aircraft, and a tacit trade in offsetting unilateral reductions of American nuclear warheads and Soviet armored forces during 1980.

It is something of a paradox that, after decades of effort by the East to negotiate limits on American forward-based nuclear weapons, talks on European nuclear forces are finally convened because of West German concerns about Soviet medium-range missiles. These concerns are as much political as military, but now that talks are underway they will have to deal largely with technical problems, in particular how to assess the balance of forces under consideration.

The European Nuclear Balance

Military capabilities depend on many unquantifiable variables such as military training, political will, technological sophistication, and geographical asym-

65

metries. Soviet and NATO nuclear forces were developed on different schedules to meet the different security needs of a totalitarian power defending a large continental landmass, and a maritime alliance of pluralistic democracies defending geographically scattered territories. Not surprisingly, these forces cannot easily be balanced quantitatively, despite an overall parity in deterrent capability.[1]

In the mid-1950s, NATO adopted a nuclear-defense policy to compensate for a perceived Soviet superiority in conventional forces. Over the next decade and a half the United States deployed thousands of short-range nuclear weapons in Western Europe. To threaten Soviet territory directly, the United States deployed a fleet of nuclear-capable aircraft at forward bases and on carriers around the Soviet perimeter. Intermediate-range land-based cruise and ballistic missiles were also deployed in Western Europe in the wake of Sputnik, but only as a temporary measure (pending development of an American intercontinental-range missile) and they were withdrawn in the late 1960s as Polaris Submarine–launched ballistic missiles were assigned to SACEUR for NATO missions. By the 1970s, NATO's nuclear arsenal comprised a modest British force of Polaris SLBMs, medium-range Vulcan bombers, and shorter range Buccaneer strike aircraft—fully integrated into NATO strike plans—plus an American NATO-assigned force of several hundred Polaris SLBMs and carrier-based aircraft and somewhere between 7,000 and 10,000 warheads for use on land-based systems, demolition mines, and a variety of short-range missiles and artillery pieces.[2]

For obvious command and control reasons, the Soviet Union has placed less emphasis on short-range battlefield nuclear weapons and long-range manned bombers. It has been much less willing to share control of nuclear systems with any of its allies. The earliest Soviet nuclear efforts focused on medium-range missiles and bombers to counter the NATO nuclear threat from Western Europe in the 1950s. Through the 1960s, aircraft development was deemphasized in favor of missiles. The intermediate-range–missile force was maintained even after development of Soviet intercontinental missiles. Not until the late 1960s and early 1970s did the Soviets refocus on sophisticated fighter aircraft; they still have nothing to compare with American carrier-based aircraft and have only recently developed nuclear artillery. Few, if any, nuclear warheads are deployed in Eastern Europe. All the nuclear-artillery pieces and many of the shorter-range Scuds, Frogs, and Scaleboards are deployed in the Western military districts of the Soviet Union, well back from the NATO border. These systems are either intended to deter a NATO advance into Eastern Europe or would have to be brought forward at the start of any NATO Pact nuclear engagement.

Since sound defense planning does not require matching forces across the board with the adversary, for two decades nuclear asymmetries between East and West were relatively tolerable to both sides. For example, far from trying to counter Soviet superiority in intermediate-range missiles in Europe, the

United States withdrew analogous systems (Thor and Jupiter ballistic, Mace and Matador cruise) in favor of less vulnerable submarine-launched Polaris. This emphasized rather than corrected existing asymmetries.

For the purpose of negotiating formal limits at the Geneva talks, however, European nuclear balances are likely to be measured in static quantifiable units, an artificial and difficult exercise even when conducted in good faith. It is also one which inevitably reduces tolerance for asymmetries and generates pressures to correct newly perceived imbalances. The decision to exclude the SS-20 and the Backfire bomber from SALT II limits, for example, served to focus attention on the threat that both systems posed for Europe and to generate pressure for analogous NATO systems—despite the fact that the overall military balance had not changed. Furthermore, Soviet efforts to ban the transfer of cruise-missile technology suggested to the NATO allies, that Soviet-American arms control could deny Western Europe useful defense technologies.

On the other hand, one of the most successful achievements of the SALT II agreement was the establishment of an agreed-on data base on Soviet and American strategic nuclear-delivery vehicles and the commitment of both parties to keep the data current. Agreeing on data for European nuclear forces will be a more formidable task, however. Not only are the forces much less symmetrical, but many systems are multi-capable so that their nuclear status will be ambiguous without agreed-on monitoring and inspection procedures. In addition some systems with obvious European missions are already counted in SALT (American Poseidon missile submarines assigned to SACEUR and Soviet SS-11 and SS-19 missiles targeted on Western Europe). Most delicate of all, this is a bilateral forum that must deal with, or compensate for, the nuclear forces of at least two, possibly three, other powers.

As the Geneva talks opened in late November 1981, Soviet and American versions of the balance of forces and the scope of the proposed limitations were far apart. The Reagan administration claimed a Soviet superiority of intermediate-range nuclear forces of 6 to 1, while the Soviets asserted a rough parity with NATO in the European theater (see table 6-1). With respect to the scope of the restrictions, the Soviet Union wanted to limit a broad list of weapons systems of intermediate range (over 1,000 kilometers) in a narrowly defined geographical zone, while the United States proposed limits on the global balance of Soviet and American nuclear systems of a narrowly defined kind.

Specifically, the Soviets proposed that by 1990 the USSR and NATO reduce by one third their current inventories of approximately 1,000 systems each.[3] The initial Soviet proposal envisaged freedom to mix between sea-, air-, and land-based missiles and between different national forces. Thus, while counting British and French forces in the NATO balance, the Soviets do not specify which forces (American, British, or French) would have to be reduced.

The American opening position, based on the zero-option proposal

Table 6-1
U.S. and USSR Views of the Nuclear Balance

	U.S. View			Soviet View		
US		USSR		US + NATO		USSR
IRBM						
		SS-20	250			
		SS-4 + 5	350	French IRBM	18	SS-20	243
		SS-12/22	100	French SLBM	80	SS-4 + 5	253
	0	SS-4-5	30	U.K. Polaris	64	SS-N-5	18
Bombers						
				F-111	172		
F-111				FB-111	65		
in Europe	164	Backfire Tu-26	45	F-4	246		
FB-111		Blinder Tu-22	350	A-6	240		
in U.S.	63	Badger Tu-16		A-7			
F-4	265	Su-17		French Mirage		Backfire Tu-26	
A-6	68	Su-24	2,700	IVA	46	Blinder Tu-22	461
A-7		Mig-27		U.K. Vulcan	55	Badger Tu-16	
Total	560		3,825		986		975

Sources: *The New York Times,* November 30, 1981, and interview material, Geneva, December 1981.

Note that the U.S. view ignores its own Pershing IA while counting analogous SS-12/22 missiles on the Soviet side and includes all Soviet Frontal Aviation as nuclear-capable but ignores much of NATO nuclear-capable tactical aircraft. The Soviet view assumes A6s and A7s on all six U.S. aircraft carriers available to Europe and includes NATO short-range systems but excludes its own tactical aircraft.

announced by President Reagan on November 18, 1981, was presented in Geneva in early February 1982 as a draft treaty. The United States would agree to cancel its long-range theater nuclear-force modernization approved by NATO ministers in December 1979—which would replace 108 Pershing IA missiles with longer-range Pershing IIs and 464 older shorter-range missiles with 464 longer-range ground-launched cruise missiles—in exchange for the dismantling of all Soviet SS-20, SS-4, and SS-5 missiles, and a freeze at current levels of the shorter-range SS-21, SS-22, and SS-23 missiles.

Alternative Negotiating Approaches

Tables 6-2, 6-3, and 6-4 showing short-, medium-, and intermediate-range nuclear forces stationed in and targeted on Europe, indicate that, while

Prospects for Limiting Nuclear Forces

Table 6–2
IRBMs and Medium-Range Nuclear-Capable Aircraft

Intermediate-Range Ballistic Missiles[a]						Medium-Range Nuclear-Capable Aircraft					
NATO		China		USSR		NATO		China		USSR	
						UK Vulcan	57			Backfire	
						UK Buccanner	60			Tu-26	135
				SS-20	243[d]	French Mirage				Blinder	
UK SLBM	64			SS-4	350	IVA	33			Tu-22	165
French SLBM	80	IRBM	70	SS-5		US F-111	164			Badger	
French IRBM	18	MRBM	50	SS-N-5	39	US FB-111	63	B-6	90	Tu-16	580
Total	162		120[b]		632		377		90		880[c]

Source: *Military Balance* 1981-1982 (London: IISS, 1981); *The New York Times*, November 30, 1981

[a] 1,000-5,000 kilometer range

[b] China also has ICBMs

[c] Of these, 70 Backfire, 40 Blinders and 270 Badgers are Soviet Naval Air Force bombers.

[d] The U.S. Department of State estimates Soviet SS-20 deployments at 300 as of March 16, 1982. Leonid Zamyatin, a member of the Central Committee of the Soviet Communist Party, claims that no additional SS-20s have been deployed since November 1981.

Table 6–3
Short-Range Nuclear-Capable Strike Aircraft

NATO		USSR	
United States		*USSR-Based*	
F-4 (US based)	800	Su-7 Fitter A	165
F-4 (Eur. based)	204	MiG 21 Fishbed J/N	750
F-4 (carrier)	144[a]	MiG 27 Flogger D	500
A-6	60[a]	Su-17 Fitter C/D	740
A-7	144[a]	Su-19-24 Fencer	480
NATO-Europe		*East Europe-Based*	
U.K. Jaguar	>80	Fitter aircraft	150
French Jaguar			
French Etendard	36		
French Mirage IIIE	30		
FRG, Greek,			
Turkish F-4	180		
F-104	318		
Total	1,996		2,785

[a] Assumes six aircraft carriers available in Europe.

Table 6-4
Tactical Nuclear-Delivery Vehicles

NATO		USSR	
U.S. Systems in Europe		USSR	
Pershing 1A SRBM	108	Scaleboard SRBM	
Lance SRBM	36	SS-12/SS-22	130
203mm artillery	56	Scud SRBM	
155mm artillery	252	SS-1//SS-23	540
		FROG SRBM	
U.S. systems under double		SS-21	668
key with European Forces		S-23 artillery	168
Honest John SRBM	42		
Pershing IA SRBM	72		
Lance SRBM	61		
203mm artillery	202		
155mm artillery	1,402		
French systems			
Pluton SRBM	42		
Total	2,273		1,506

Note: Less than 1,000-kilometer range

imbalances exist in selected categories, an overall East-West parity prevails. In this situation, stability might best be maintained by a mutual moratorium on additional nuclear forces and tacit understandings to tolerate existing asymmetries. Until Soviet-American and intra-NATO relations improve, however, tacit understandings are neither likely to satisfy political leaders looking for equitable, verifiable arms control agreements, nor reassure publics looking for signs of real progress toward disarmament. Drawing on the lessons of earlier arms control experience, at least four different negotiating approaches are worth exploring: the status quo, the status quo ante, the SALT-plus, and the comprehensive.

The Status-Quo Approach

If we have learned anything from the past three decades of arms control diplomacy, it is that prolonged negotiations are net consumers of trust and confidence between political adversaries. An early agreement to codify mutually acceptable aspects of the status quo should preclude lengthy debates about setting new ceilings, avoid the acquisition of extra forces as bargaining chips, and prevent the rechannelling of arms production from limited to unlimited systems. The ideal status quo agreement would be to select packages of forces in which an obviously equitable balance currently exists, that would be threatened by deployment of proposed new systems. At first sight, table 6-2 suggests that intermediate range ballistic missiles are hopelessly out of balance, with 632 Soviet systems and only 282 for NATO and China combined. Since it is the new SS–20s that concern West Europeans, however, rather than the early SS–4s and SS–5s, these older systems could be either dismantled or discounted for the sake of forging an agreement. At December 1981 levels of 243 SS–20s, total Soviet IRBMS would balance IRBM threats to the Soviet Union from Britain, France, and China, 282 to 282.[4]

One obvious problem with this package, as with the opening Soviet position requiring NATO to cut its combined intermediate-range force by a third, is that neither France, Britain, nor China is party to the Geneva talks, so that the imposition of a ceiling of, say 280, on Soviet IRBMs would have to be balanced on the Western side by a freeze, not only on new American deployments, but also on French, British, and Chinese strategic systems. Another drawback is that such a status-quo agreement would not reduce the current level of SS–20s and may not adequately meet the concerns of those who fear the SS–20s as a qualitatively new military threat. Newly deployed forces are not easily relinquished, however, so the chances of dismantling SS–20s seem remote A firm ceiling on current deployments should at least ease the fears of those such as Chancellor Schmidt, who see the Soviets using their growing preponderance in IRBMs to exert political pressure.

Another potential component of a status-quo package could balance Soviet and NATO medium-range nuclear-capable bombers. The Soviet Union claims a NATO superiority of 700 to 410 in these systems.[5] According to IISS figures, however, (table 6-2) Soviet long-range aviation currently deploys some 880 nuclear-capable aircraft, while NATO plus China deploys 467 aircraft of similar range and capability. Again, at first glance, this looks like a formidable Soviet superiority, but the Soviets could denuclearize their 580 (1955-vintage) Badger bombers, their nuclear-capable medium-range bombers would be reduced to 300 systems facing a NATO (without China) capability of 377. NATO could be brought well within a ceiling of 300 by denuclearizing either or both the British Vulcans or Buccaneers, something that is scheduled for the near future in any event.[6]

Fashioning an obviously equitable package of shorter-range nuclear-capable aircraft looks more difficult. Under SALT counting rules, any system once tested in a nuclear mode would count as a nuclear-capable system in any agreed to limits. Thus the Soviet–NATO ratio of shorter-range nuclear-capable aircraft would approximate 2.8 to 2 (2,785 to 1,996 in table 6-3). Almost certainly, however, many if not most, of these systems do not have assigned nuclear missions, even though theoretically nuclear capable. The opportunity costs of training crews for nuclear, rather than conventional, missions are acknowledged to be very high for NATO air forces, and we can assume the same holds true for the Soviets. The Geneva talks could thus perform a useful arms-control purpose by making a virtue out of necessity and establishing verifiable procedures for formally denuclearizing aircraft. This might take the form of installing functionally related observable differences (FRODS), monitoring training sorties that are different for nuclear and conventional missions, and setting up schemes for the inspections of ammunition sites or for verifying nuclear-free air bases. Such measures would not only reduce the risk of escalation to nuclear war by miscalculation, but would also serve to shore up the conventional deterrent on both sides, presumably making any agreement more acceptable to the military establishments of both East and West.

It should be noted that there has already been considerable unilateral denuclearization of NATO aircraft, and that more is scheduled in connection with the NATO double decision of December 1979, which requires that for each new ground-launched cruise missile (GLCM) deployed, one old warhead must be withdrawn. Harold Brown, Secretary of Defense under President Carter, suggested that GLCMs could replace nuclear bombs currently allocated to dual-capable aircraft in Europe, so as to free up these systems to fly conventional missions.[7]

From the Soviet perspective, replacing one American nuclear warhead with another may not seem much like arms control. A more attractive, and posibly negotiable option might be to ban all nuclear-armed GLCMs, but allow NATO to deploy 464 conventionally armed cruise missiles to replace nuclear bombs currently assigned to forward-based aircraft. This would have the important political advantage for NATO of maintaining the form of the December 1979 double decision.

The Status-Quo-Ante Approach

Just as NATO plans for new nuclear deployments in the 1950s and 1960s generated pressure for the establishment of nuclear free zones (NFZs) in Europe, so NATO's December 1979 decision to modernize its nuclear arsenal brought forth a new crop of proposals for Nordic, Balkan, and Central European nuclear free zones in the early 1980s. Proponents argue that NFZs would supplement the current NPT regime by preventing one country from storing the nuclear weapons of another.[8] The ultimate status-quo-ante agreement would revert to the 1940s and a nuclear-free Europe, as proposed by the European Nuclear Disarmament (END) movement. No one expects anything so radical to emerge from the Geneva talks of course, and the reports of nuclear material aboard the Soviet submarine stranded off the Swedish coast in October 1981 took some of the steam out of the pressure building for a Nordic nuclear-free zone. Interest could no doubt be revived if the zone were redefined to include the Baltic and the Kola peninsulas, but these are provisions the Soviets have been unwilling to entertain in the past.[9]

Prospects for Limiting Nuclear Forces 73

The most extreme status-quo-ante proposal under serious consideration in Geneva is President Reagan's zero option, which has the enthusiastic endorsement of Chancellor Schmidt and official NATO support, but rather more qualified approval from Britain's conservative government, where some defense analysts still believe NATO needs to modernize its intermediate-range nuclear forces regardless of Soviet systems. The Reagan zero option seems designed primarily to put the onus of NATO's modernization program on the Soviet Union, rather than as a serious proposal. It would mean, in effect, returning to the status quo of 1956, a time before the Soviet Union had deployed any medium-range missiles, and when the NATO powers had an overwhelming superiority of short-range systems.

A more reasonable approach would be to return to the status quo prior to the NATO-modernization decision in late 1979, when Mr. Brezhnev declared parity between Soviet and NATO medium-range missiles. Many Western analysts argue that if parity existed in October 1979, it can hardly be said to still hold through the period during which only the Soviet Union continued to deploy new hardware, while NATO merely pursued missile development. On his November 1981 visit to Bonn, Mr. Brezhnev suggested a Soviet willingness to withdraw hundreds of intermediate-range missiles. Presumably he referred to old SS–4s and SS–5s, as well as the new SS–20s. Some NATO allies have suggested that reduction back to the approximately one hundred SS–20s deployed in October 1979 would be sufficient to warrant cancellation of the new NATO missiles. Others would permit the Soviets to deploy up to 244 SS–20 missiles so long as all the SS–4s and SS–5s were dismantled.[10] This would give the Soviets approximately the same number of warheds on medium-range missiles as were deployed on SS–4s and SS–5s at their maximum level in 1964–1965.[11]

The SALT-Plus Approach

Through the spring of 1982, the Reagan administration cited the imposition of martial law in Poland as the reason for delaying a new round of strategic-arms-reduction talks (START). Even as the START talks opened, the relationship between the Geneva talks on European nuclear forces and START was still unclear. At the NATO meeting in Rome in May 1981, then Secretary of State Haig linked the two forums, as he did again in September when he met with Soviet Foreign Minister Gromyko to set the date for the European talks. There has been little in the declaratory arms control policy of the Reagan administration, however, to suggest any continuity with the SALT Treaty signed in June 1979, an agreement that President Reagan has described as "fatally flawed" and that former Secretary of State Haig pronounced "dead."

Nevertheless pressure grew in mid-1982 for ratification of SALT II to precede the new START negotiations. One obvious cost of not ratifying the treaty by January 1, 1982, was the fact that the Soviets were under no legal obligation to dismantle strategic launchers to reach the SALT II ceilings of 2,250, as they would have been had the treaty been in force. In other respects though, the treaty provisions were being observed and several analysts have suggested using the SALT II framework as the basis for limiting intermediate-range systems. Lawrence Freedman proposed raising the limit currently imposed on Soviet and American central (intercontinental) systems to accommodate 400 medium-range systems each for both the United States and the Soviet Union.[12] SALT could then limit American forward-based systems, a persistent Soviet objective since the very first negotiating session in November 1969. In exchange, the Soviets would have to accept SALT limits on their own analogous systems: the SS–20s, SS–4s, and SS–5s as well as the Backfire, Badger, and Blinder bombers. An obvious difficulty with this scheme is that a limit of 400 would not accommodate shorter-range nuclear-capable fighter aircraft, and there might then be a tendency for these systems to proliferate if they were the only nuclear-capable elements unlimited by treaty. This suggests the need for more drastic reductions, or a higher limit than 400, or a denuclearizing of dual-capable systems as proposed above.

William Hyland, a defense analyst in the Nixon, Ford, and Carter administrations and a major architect of the SALT II agreement, proposed a first-phase agreement in which Soviet SS–20 missiles are offset by Pershing I and Pershing II missiles in West Germany.[13] Hyland suggests that the Soviets reduce their force of SS–20s to about 65, thus implying a warhead count of approximately 200, which could then be offset by an equivalent number of Pershing I and II missiles in West Germany. This arrangement would accommodate all the 108 proposed new extended-range Pershing II missiles and the existing seventy-two Pershing IA missiles deployed under double-key control with West German forces. The idea of controlling German-held weapons should have some appeal to the Soviets, but a more attractive version of this proposal for arms-control advocates would be to reduce the SS–20s to sixty (180 warheads) and consider these to be offset by current Pershing I deployments. The next phase of Hyland's plan would incorporate all cruise missiles in new SALT ceilings. Again, this is a concept that may appeal to the Soviets since, at best, it offers the opportunity to forestall deployment of American ground-launched cruise missiles in Western Europe (the December 1979 plan), and to preclude deployment of new submarine-launched cruise missiles on attack submarines as proposed by President Reagan in 1981. It is almost certainly too late to prevent deployment of American air-launched cruise missiles, but at least these are limited by the (albeit unratified) SALT II Treaty.

At this writing it is not clear whether NATO governments would be uniformly in favor of a ban on sea- and ground-launched cruise missiles. As noted earlier, during the SALT II negotiations, Soviet efforts to ban the transfer of cruise-missile technology were strenuously opposed by a small but influential coterie of American and West European defense analysts that argued that a ban on cruise would deny France and Britain useful strategic-follow-on possibilities, and deny all West European defense establishments potentially useful nonnuclear-defense technologies. Since that time many other analysts on both sides of the Atlantic have emphasized the flaws in cruise technology as well as the serious strategic and arms-race instabilities that could arise if both East and West deploy nuclear cruise. In addition, a ground swell of opposition to the deployment of new GLCMs in Western Europe is forcing governments to reconsider their acquiescence to the December 1979 decision and reweigh the pros and cons of cruise for NATO defense.[14]

The Comprehensive Approach

Table 6-4 shows NATO and Soviet land-based nuclear-capable systems under the 1,000-kilometer range. Until the late 1970s, NATO had a monopoly in nuclear artillery and it still retains an overwhelming superiority—more than 1,900 pieces—over Soviet ground forces that only deploy 168 pieces, all of which are deployed in the Western military districts of the Soviet Union.[15] The Soviets have the edge in nuclear-capable missiles in the 50–1,000-kilometer range with 1,338 Scuds, Frogs, and Scaleboards, of which some 375–400 are deployed in the Far East. NATO plus France deploy 361 analogous systems in Western Europe: Pershing IA, Lance, Honest John, and the Pluton. The actual balance of nuclear capability is particularly difficult to assess in these systems, since only the Pershings and the Pluton are unambiguously nuclear; all the other NATO and Soviet systems are multi-capable with the option of carrying high-explosive, chemical, or nuclear warheads. Other land-based short-range nuclear systems in Europe include Soviet and American air-defense missiles and American atomic demolition mines (ADMs). These mines were intended, but apparently never so deployed, for use as a nuclear trip-wire on the NATO–Warsaw Pact borders.

The case for including short-range systems in a comprehensive across-the-board ceiling on all nuclear forces in Europe rests on the fact, as mentioned earlier, that piecemeal arms-control treaties often encourage military establishments to acquire extra strength in categories of weapons not limited by the agreements. Thus if the Geneva talks set limits only on intermediate-range land-based missiles and aircraft, there would be a tendency to upgrade battlefield and submarine-launched systems. Indeed, these pressures were already evident in the Reagan FY 1983-defense budget, which calls for production of the neutron bomb and for hundreds of submarine-launched cruise missiles on American attack submarines.[16]

Including short-range missiles and nuclear artillery in the negotiations would be something of a mixed blessing, however, since these systems would then become important as bargaining chips. There have already been suggestions in the American defense literature that the negotiations in Vienna and Geneva should be used to rationalize an upgrading of NATO battlefield-nuclear weapons, specifically to match the SS–21, SS–22 and SS–23, which are replacing the older Frog, Scaleboard, and Scud missiles in the Soviet Union and Eastern Europe.[17]

Concern about the upgrading of Soviet short-range systems is certainly legitimate, but matching each new Soviet development may not be the optimum solution. On the contrary, many Western defense analysts argue that nuclear-battlefield weapons serve no useful military purpose, complicate the task of conventional defense in Europe, and ought to be unilaterally withdrawn or denuclearized.[18] Short-range nuclear weapons are destabilizing, primarily because they are deployed so far forward that they risk being overcome, or used, very early in any military conflict. The arms control paradox here is that an attempt to negotiate a comprehensive agreement on European nuclear forces might preclude unilateral withdrawal of these systems.

If so, it would not be the first time that arms control diplomacy had interfered with sound defense planning. American Titan ICBMs, for example, were retained as bargaining chips at SALT long after they would otherwise have been due for retirement. Only in late 1981, after two serious accidents, did the Defense Department order these systems to be dismantled. Similarly, during the mid-1970s, when Greece and Turkey were at loggerheads over Cyprus, there was considerable pressure in the United States Congress and Defense Department to remove American nuclear weapons from what was seen as NATO's volatile southern flank, and for removing obsolete nuclear systems from central Europe at the same time. In contrast to the withdrawal of Thor, Jupiter, Mace, and Matador missiles by Secretary MacNamara in the 1960s, proposals to remove obsolete nuclear weapons from the continent in the 1970s were blocked by the State Department on the grounds that removing NATO weapons would be squandering valuable bargaining chips at the MBFR negotiations with the Warsaw Pact in Vienna. (One can imagine similar debates in Moscow about the virtues of retaining SS–4s and SS–5s as bargaining chips in the current Geneva talks.)

In December 1975, NATO's Option III proposal in Vienna offered to withdraw thirty-six Pershing IA missile launchers, fifty-four F–4 nuclear-capable aircraft and one thousand nuclear warheads, in exchange for withdrawal of a Soviet tank army. The Soviets countered in February 1976 with a more symmetrical proposal: to withdraw equal numbers of U.S. Pershing IA and Soviet Scud missiles, equal numbers of Soviet Fitter aircraft and F–4s, equal numbers of nuclear air-defense missiles SAM–2s and Nike Hercules, and equal numbers of nuclear warheads. This proposal was unacceptable to NATO, and Option III was subsequently withdrawn.

Since that time, however, both sides have withdrawn unilaterally some of the systems included in these earlier proposals. The Soviets have withdrawn 20,000 troops and 1,000 tanks from East Germany, and the United States has withdrawn 1,000 obsolete nuclear warheads and denuclearized some aircraft. In April 1981, NATO ministers agreed to withdraw several hundred obsolete Nike Hercules air-defense missiles and atomic-demolition mines in the near future.[19] It will be interesting to observe the impact of the Geneva talks on the implementation of these decisions.

Conclusion

The fragility of East-West detente, and the growing pressure to deploy provocative new counterforce weapons, makes nuclear arms control more urgent than ever before. The Geneva talks on European nuclear forces began on a serious note in November 1981 with both sides maintaining professional silence on each other's proposals. After the imposition of martial law in Poland, however, the atmosphere in Geneva appeared to deteriorate as both sides took their latest negotiating positions to the public, suggesting tht propoganda-making had become a more important objective than arms control. In May 1982, the Reagan administration made public a proposal for strategic-arms reductions considerably more radical and more demanding of the Soviets than the SALT II agreement signed in June 1979, again more suggestive of propoganda than of serious policy.[20]

This chapter suggests that a number of equitable packages of European nuclear forces are negotiable and that the least costly approach—in terms of political tensions generated, new weapons rationalized, and obsolete systems retained—would be to fashion a simple status-quo agreement as soon as possible. Ideally, such an agreement would establish a standing consultative commission on European nuclear forces, not only to monitor the basic agreement but also to address each side's long-term security needs with a view to preventing the deployment of destabilizing new systems and, eventually, to generate the necessary degree of mutual trust and confidence that will permit substantial force reductions.[21]

Success will depend primarily on political will and, at a minimum, will require insulating the Geneva talks from other aspects of East-West and Soviet-American competition. A crucial factor will be how the newly aroused antinuclear movements conduct themselves. Many observers see President Reagan's modification of the MX-missile program, his adoption of a zero option for intermediate-range missiles, and the new START proposals, as pragmatic responses to these politically broad-based-protest movements in the United States and Western Europe. Sustained pressure from these constituencies could have a significant impact on the American negotiating position.

Notes

1. For analyses that judged Soviet and NATO theater-nuclear forces in Europe to be in rough parity before the Geneva negotiations, see "The Balance of Theater Nuclear Forces in Europe," *The Military Balance 1979–1980* (London: International Institute for Strategic Studies, 1979), pp. 114–117; Paul M. Doty and Robert Metzger, "Arms Control Enters the Grey Area," *International Security* 3, no. 3 (Winter 1978–1979).

2. While presumably deployed primarily to deter the Soviet Union, the French nuclear arsenal—comprising Mirage strike aircraft, submarine-launched ballistic missiles, land-based medium-range ballistic missiles, and the shorter-range Pluton missile—is independent of NATO for command and control purposes.

3. John Burns, "Brezhnev Offers Deep Arms Cut in Europe by '90,'" *The New York Times,* February 4, 1982.

4. The U.S. Department of State estimated Soviet SS–20 deployments at 300 on March 16, 1982. At the same time Leonid Zamyatin, a member of the CPSU Central Committee claimed that no additional SS–20 missiles had been deployed since November 1981. *The New York Times,* March 17, 1982.

5. *The Baltimore Sun,* November 21, 1981.

6. Vulcan bombers used in the raids on the Falkland Islands in early 1982 had been refitted for conventional munitions.

7. Harold Brown, *Annual Report F.Y. 1981* (Washington, D.C.: Department of Defense, January 29, 1980), pp. 148, 301.

8. Sverre Lodgaard, "A Nuclear Weapon Free Zone in the North? A Reappraisal," *The Bulletin of Peace Proposals* (Oslo) no. 1 (1980): 33–39; Randy J. Rydell and Athanassios Platias, "The Balkans: A Weapon Free Zone?" *The Bulletin of the Atomic Scientists* (May 1982): 59. For a summary of recent nuclear-weapons-free-zone proposals, see Chalmers Hardenburgh, editor, *The Arms Control Reporter: A Chronicle of Treaties, Negotiations and Proposals,* sections 404–406 (Brookline, Mass.: Institute for Defense and Disarmament, 1982) (The *Reporter* is brought up to date monthly).

9. Milton Leitenberg, "The Stranded U.S.S.R. Submarine in Sweden and the Question of a Nordic Nuclear Free Zone" *Cooperation and Conflict,* 22 (1982): 17–28.

10. For different interpretations of the zero option, see "Holding It Together," *The Economist* (November 14, 1981) and *The Washington Post,* November 8, 1981.

11. William Hyland, "Soviet Theater Nuclear Forces and Arms Control" *Survival,* 23, no. 5 (September/October 1981): 194–199.

12. Lawrence Freedman, "The Dilemma of Theater Nuclear Arms Control," *Survival,* 23, no. 1 September/October 1981): 2–10.

13. Hyland, "Soviet Theater."

14. For a thorough analysis of the pros and cons of cruise, see Richard K. Betts, editor, *Cruise Missiles: Technology, Strategy and Politics* (Washington, D.C.: The Brookings Institution, 1981).

15. International Institute for Strategic Studies, *The Military Balance 1981-1982* (London: IISS 1981), p. 107.

16. Richard D. Delauer. *The FY 1982 Department of Defense Program for Research Development and Acquisition* Statement to the 97th Congress, 2nd Session, March 2, 1982 Washington, D.C.: Department of Defense, 1982 pp. VII-7/8. Caspar Weinberger, *Annual Report to Congress F.Y. 1983* Washington, D.C.: Department of Defense, 1982, pp. 1-41.

17. See, for example, John G. Kelleher, "Ground Force Nuclear Weapons for Arms Control" in the Harvard CSIA volume on European Nuclear Forces, forthcoming.

18. See, in particular, testimony in *Nuclear Weapons and Foreign Policy,* Hearings before the Committee on Foreign Relations, United States Senate 93rd Congress (Washington, D.C.: U.S. Government Printing Office 1974); Herbert York "Balance of Terror in Europe" *The Bulletin of The Atomic Scientists* 32, no. 5 (May, 1976): 8-17. Lawrence Freedman, "NATO Myths," *Foreign Policy* no. 45 (Winter 1981-1982). Louis Mountbatten, "A Military Commander Surveys the Arms Race," *International Security*, 4, no. 3 (Winter 1979-1980).

19. Walter Pincus, *The Washington Post* November 1 and 5, 1981.

20. The new START proposals were announced in a speech by President Reagan at Eureka College, Illinois, May 10, 1982. See "Text of President Reagan's Address on Nuclear Policy and East-West Ties," *The New York Times,* May 10, 1982; and Alexander Haig "The Strategic Arms Reduction Talks," *Department of State Current Policy #389,* Washington, D.C.: State Department Bureau of Public Affairs, May 11, 1982.

21. For a discussion of the potential of the SALT Standing Consultative Commission, see, Jane M.O. Sharp "Restructuring the SALT Dialogue," *International Security* 6, no. 3 (Winter 1981-82).

Intermediate-Nuclear-Force Negotiations: Issues and Alternatives

Gregory F. Treverton

Background to Current Negotiations

Events of the last few years have reawakened an old concern in the NATO alliance: the role of nuclear weapons in Europe, especially those with range enough to reach the Soviet Union, now called LRTNF or INF, terms used interchangeably here. The issue is as old as the alliance, running back to the debate in the 1950s over the role of what were then called medium- (or intermediate-) range ballistic missiles (M/IRBMs) in Europe.[1] The United States deployed sixty Thor IRBMs in Britain and forty-five Jupiters in Italy and Turkey beginning in the late 1950s; yet those deployments were viewed from the start by the United States as a stopgap: once intercontinental ballistic missiles in the United States could cover all the Soviet targets of interest, the need for the IRBMs would fade. With the rapid buildup of American ICBM forces in the early 1960s, the IRBMs were withdrawn by 1964.

By contrast, from the beginning Soviet actions suggest a strong interest in having systems to target both the United States and Western Europe. The Soviet Union began deploying large numbers of SS-4 and SS-5 missiles targeted on Western Europe in the late 1950s. At that point, the Soviet deployment against Europe served in part as a hedge against technical problems in Soviet ICBM programs: the Soviets evidently decided to wait to deploy second-generation ICBMs in the late 1960s, and the IRBM deployments served to hold Europe hostage against American nuclear superiority in the interim. Yet the Soviet Union retained large deployments against Western Europe even once its strategic arsenal equalled that of the United States, clear testimony that Soviet IRBMs were not a stopgap measure.

The debate over what are now called INF subsided for more than a decade after 1965. The East-West climate was warming, and the early successes of arms control fed hopes for more. At least as important, the rapid American nuclear buildup produced a U.S. superiority that, psychologically at least, seemed to mean that it did not matter much that Europe remained hostage to Soviet missiles targeted against it. A combination of factors revived concern about INF in the late 1970s: the Soviet conventional buildup continued apace, and the Soviet Union began deploying a new generation of INF, especially the highly accurate, three-warhead SS-20; more important, Soviet strategic-force improvements made the Soviet Union at least the nuclear equal of the United

81

82 Nuclear Weapons in Europe

Figure 7–1. Soviet SS–4 Missile

Intermediate-Nuclear-Force Negotiations

Figure 7-2. Soviet SS-5 Missile

Figure 7–3. Soviet SS–20 Missile

States, a parity codified in SALT II, which also directed attention to the INF balance because those systems were excluded from the treaty. West German Chancellor Schmidt brought the issue into the public view in October 1977 in a speech in London. He said: "SALT neutralizes ... strategic nuclear capabilities. In Europe this magnifies the significance of the disparities between East and West in nuclear tactical and conventional weapons."[2]

The INF issue obviously touched the heart of NATO strategy, and the Alliance went through a painstaking two-year process of analysis beginning even before the Schmidt speech. That analysis was conducted within two parallel bodies, both of which involved senior experts from NATO capitals—the so-called High Level Group on the military side, and the Special Group, later the Special Consultative Group, to deal with arms control. The result was the double decision of December 1979.[3] The alliance would deploy in Western Europe 572 American cruise and Pershing II ballistic missiles capable of reaching the Soviet Union, beginning in 1983. At the same time, NATO committed itself to pursue, in bilateral Soviet-American negotiations "in the SALT II framework," negotiated limits on INF.

Preliminary Soviet-American negotiations began in Geneva in September 1980, notwithstanding the shelving of SALT II in the wake of the Soviet invasion of Afghanistan. Their future was cast into doubt by the American election and by uncertainties over President Reagan's attitude to nuclear-arms control, but the new administration soon committed itself to continuing the Geneva negotiations. The talks resumed at the end of November 1981, again despite the uncertainties over the future of the SALT (or START) talks, an issue to be discussed below.

Politics and Military Strategy

Discussion of both INF deployments and arms control is often murky because political and military considerations are so intertwined. NATO strategy has always confronted a nuclear dilemma that cannot be washed away: Europe is dependent, finally, on the American strategic deterrent, most of which is on the other side of the Atlantic from the point of attack. The role of NATO's nuclear forces in Europe always has been vague, with Europeans tending to view them as a link or trigger to American strategic forces, and Americans conceiving them as a complement to conventional defense if need be. INF have been both the most difficult to conceptualize in military terms—at what point would they be used, against which targets, and why INF instead of American central systems?—and the most sensitive politically, since they mean striking the USSR.

In these circumstances, the role of INF, as deterrence in general, must be both political and military. The credibility of the American nuclear guarantee to Western Europe is primarily a matter of political cohesion, an awareness of shared stakes backed by the presence of 300,000 American GIs in Europe. Weapons matter, but politics are decisive. In particular, the general state of the transatlantic relationship will bear on the political adequacy of nuclear arrangements as much as on the specifics of military hardware. When Europeans are tolerably confident of American purpose and leadership, nuclear matters will be less salient; when they are not, specific issues, such as the SS–20, will emerge as surrogates for concern about the ultimate reliability of the American nuclear guarantee.

To view INF either in purely military or purely political terms is to misconstrue its purpose. A purely military view would denigrate the 572 proposed missiles as too few and of too dubious survivability to matter. Those are not arguments that can be dismissed out of hand, but they do underestimate the value weaponry can have in adding credibility to strategic arrangements that depend primarily on political factors. On the other hand, to view INF as purely political, without any military purpose, is to risk the opposite error. If proposed force deployments, driven by political considerations, are unconvincing on their military merits to the ostensible military experts, they will not serve the political purposes for which they are intended. That is a critical lesson of the multilateral force (MLF) episode of the 1960s. The MLF was to be a fleet of NATO surface ships, manned by sailors of different nations, carrying nuclear missiles whose warheads would be under U.S. control. Yet MLF was not convincing to military experts; that, in the end, made it unattractive to politicians. If the military argument for deploying the 572 missiles is unconvincing, they should not be deployed, for they will not serve the essentially political objective of strengthening the credibility of NATO's deterrent. Thus the military rationale for the new systems is crucial.

Negotiating a Balance from Imbalance

Against this backdrop, the overriding puzzle in the Geneva negotiations is how they could be used to create a balance where none now exists. Soviet LRTNF or INF systems that are the subject of first concern, as the SS–20 missile, are many and increasing rapidly to number—250 SS–20s at the beginning of 1982, with fifty to sixty additional systems being deployed annually—while NATO is still two years away from beginning to deploy comparable systems, the 572 long-range cruise missiles and Pershing II ballistic missiles decided in December 1979. The existing balance in modern land-based long-range theater missiles, the category on which NATO has focused, is thus 250 to zero in the Soviet favor (or 250 to eighteen, if the eighteen French SSBS S–2 missiles are included on the Western side).

Hence NATO is in the position of bargaining its intentions—and intentions that European opposition to nuclear weapons may make dubious at that—against Soviet systems in place. Little in logic suggests that the USSR will have much incentive to accede to an agreement that would produce anything like parity; little in the history of arms control provides ground for a more hopeful conclusion. Despite the painstaking process of consultations in alliance history, the commitment to arms control in that decision was driven by political considerations: given the distaste for the nuclear in Europe, a serious effort at arms control was deemed necessary if NATO was to have any chance of actually deploying the 572 missiles. NATO is thus saddled with negotiations that are politically imperative but technically unpromising in the extreme. Its position is similar to that with which it entered the Mutual and Balanced Force Reduction (MBFR) talks in Vienna in the early 1970s, but it is worse in two particulars: NATO reckons the preexisting imbalance as worse in the TNF case, and, unlike MBFR, TNF talks, which merely drag on with no result in sight, are not likely to achieve the political objectives for which they were designed.

Different constructions of the TNF balance—that is, including different categories of weapons—obviously affect the result, but no reasonable construction comes close to eliminating the puzzle. For instance, Mr. Brezhnev's assertion that there is already parity in LRTNF, with 986 Western systems to 975 Soviet—which also, and unfortunately, established the Soviet figure of 975 as a canon for Soviet negotiators—reflected a number of untenable assumptions.[4] It apparently counted a larger number of Western F–4 aircraft than exists in inventories, much less have a nuclear role. More important, Brezhnev included some Western systems (as F–4s) while excluding Soviet systems with comparable or greater capabilities (as Fencers).

Negotiating Issues

Beyond the puzzle, the United States and its European allies confront a number of thorny issues in the LRTNF negotiations, summarized here more or less in the order in which they occur:

What Relationship to SALT or START?

From the beginning, NATO has assumed that any LRTNF negotiations would take place only in tight relation to the central SALT process; indeed the December 1979 decision mentioned that context. Europeans assumed, erroneously, that SALT II would be ratified soon thereafter; nevertheless, in subsequent NATO meetings, the Europeans pressed for reaffirmation of the SALT link, and both American administrations acceded; yet clearly the future of the central-strategic negotiations is perilous. Given Poland and the state of Soviet-American relations, it is unclear when the negotiations might begin seriously. Given the apparent preference of the Reagan administration for "deep cuts," it is predictable at least that the Soviet Union will take considerable time to adjust and respond seriously to American proposals once they are made. Hence it is hard to see that serious business could be done in the strategic negotiations until 1983, even under relatively rosy assumptions about the East-West climate.

The arguments for trying to sustain a tight link between LRTNF and the central-strategic negotiations are

1. Doctrinally, NATO stresses the continuum of nuclear deterrence. In particular, the December 1979 decision on new deployments was taken explicitly to reinforce the link between the European theater and central American-strategic-nuclear forces. The link that NATO plans forces to sustain should not be weakened by arms-control approaches that seem to separate—decouple, in the jargon of the trade—strategic forces from their closest doctrinal kin, LRTNF.

2. Logically, it makes little sense to proceed too far with the LRTNF talks while the future of limits on central-strategic forces is unclear. Why, after all, strive for limits on the Soviet SS–20 if the Soviet intercontinental forces, SS–17s, SS–18s, and SS–19s may be unconstrained? Accepting these arguments means recognizing that the Geneva LRTNF talks are bound to be a holding action at best until the future of the central negotiations is much clearer.

There is an argument for going further, for merging the LRTNF and central-strategic negotiations at some point. For instance, the SALT II aggregate of 2250 might be raised to 2650 to include LRTNF, with both sides given freedom to determine the precise mix between LRTNF and central systems.[5] Constraints on warhead numbers might be achieved by including LRTNF systems under the SALT II subceilings on MIRVed launchers, perhaps expanded somewhat. This approach would underscore the doctrinal unity between LRTNF and central systems. As a practical matter, it would also mean that what are large asymmetries in LRTNF forces could become less dramatic in talks comprising both LRTNF and central weapons.

Against an effort to sustain a tight LRTNF-strategic-negotiating link stand the following arguments:

1. It may be possible. At a minimum, nuclear politics in Western Europe may mean that the LRTNF negotiations cannot hang in limbo for an extended period awaiting the serious commencement of the strategic negotiations, not, at any rate, if the December 1979 deployment decisions are to have any chance of being implemented. Progress in the LRTNF talks may have to come sooner than the tidy logic of the LRTNF-strategic-negotiating link would permit.

2. Any effort to merge the two sets of negotiations would, at best, only

produce more delay. SALT II took seven years to negotiate; the LRTNF talks will have technical complexities that run beyond even those of SALT. Putting the two together simply would bring the entire process to a standstill.

3. A variant of this argument holds that NATO might try to make a virtue of necessity. Since the LRTNF and strategic negotiations inevitably will diverge, NATO might explicitly separate them. It would then make a quick and acceptable LRTNF agreement the price of admission for the Soviet Union to the next round of strategic negotiations.[6] This, of course, presumes (probably correctly) that the Soviet Union has little reason to be interested in an LRTNF agreement that NATO could stomach, but also (and more dubiously) that the strategic negotiations, even with a United States committed to deep cuts, are a prize for which the Soviet Union would be prepared to pay in the coin of LRTNF.

4. Far from sustaining the link between the European theater and American central forces, a tight LRTNF-strategic-negotiating link might strain NATO politics. In tightly related or merged negotiations, it would be especially tempting for the Soviets to target proposals where the interests of America and Europe seem to diverge. Suppose, for example, that the Soviet Union accepted the principle of deep cuts in strategic forces, but only on the condition that the United States (and NATO) forgo deployment of the 572 Pershings and GLCMs. An American administration committed to deep cuts and focused on the strategic balance might be tempted to agree. Yet that would look to Europeans like trading European interests for American ones, thus provoking a row in the Alliance. Nothing would prevent the Soviet Union from making proposals of this sort even in separate negotiations—indeed they are predictable–but tightly linked negotiations would make them easier.

Launchers or Warheads

A second issue concerns the basic unit of account in the negotiations. If NATO seeks a parity, somehow defined, between Eastern and Western LRTNF, will that parity be based on launchers or warheads? Thus far there has been a strong consensus that warheads should be the unit of account, for strong military reasons. What matters, after all, is how many weapons can be delivered, not how many launchers do the delivering; moreover, all of the projected Western systems are single-warhead, while the Soviet SS–20 has three warheads per missile.

Still, it is important to recognize that negotiations based on warheads will raise both technical and political complications. Technically, how the bomb loads of nuclear-capable aircraft are translated into warheads is somewhat arbitrary and hard to verify. Politically, the use of warheads as the basis would depart from the SALT practice, where launchers have been the basic unit of account and where the United States had been reluctant to use warheads as the principle *numeraire,* because of both its own lead in warheads and its concern over the throw-weight of Soviet rockets. Finally, an agreement based on warheads will be still harder to come by than one based on launchers since the Soviet lead is all the greater in warheads, largely because of the SS–20: the 250 to zero Soviet lead in modern, land-based LRTNF missiles becomes 750 to zero if the count is based on warheads.

How to Treat Aircraft

This is the first of several issues of which systems to include in negotiations. It runs back to the beginning of SALT I. Then the Soviet Union insisted that SALT was about American and Soviet systems that could strike the homeland of the other, thus so-called forward-based systems (FBS)—American nuclear-capable aircraft based in Europe or in the Mediterranean that could reach the Soviet Union—also had to be included. Although the Soviets were never completely clear which American systems they meant by FBS, it was clear that by their definition there could be no Soviet FBS. In other words, they drew a distinction between Soviet systems that could strike the United States and those that could only strike the European NATO members.

In beginning the Geneva negotiations, the Soviet Union moved away from that position, but only somewhat. It now recognizes some symmetry between NATO missiles that can strike the Soviet Union from Western Europe and Soviet missiles that can strike Western Europe but not the United States; hence it is prepared, in principle at least, to discuss SS–20 limitations in exchange for the nondeployment of Pershings and GLCMs. Yet, as Brezhnev's construction of the LRTNF balance makes clear, the Soviet Union remains unprepared to extend that symmetry fully to aircraft; Brezhnev included the Western nuclear-capable Fencer, with capabilities at least as good as those of the F–4.

The arguments in favor of including some aircraft in the LRTNF negotiations are

1. Some aircraft on both sides are, by virtue of their range and performance, rather unambiguously comparable to missile systems in performing LRTNF roles—the Soviet Backfire and the American F–111s, for example. Excluding them would, at least, leave a gap in any agreement; at worst, it could channel competitions away from missile systems, which were covered, into aircraft, which were not.

2. If NATO wants to achieve limits on Soviet aircraft, such as Backfire, that have been the objects of recent concern, it will have to throw some of its own aircraft into the bargain.

The arguments against including aircraft are

1. The characteristics of particular aircraft are variable and hard to discern; hence their inclusion or exclusion can easily become particularly arbitrary. It is not easy for one side to know, much less to adequately verify through national-technical means (NTM) exactly what portion of the other side's force of a particular plane is nuclear capable, still harder to know how many of those actually would be used in the nuclear role should a war occur. Similarly, the range of particular planes is knowable only within broad margins, for it depends crucially on where the planes are based, on how much of a weapon load they carry and on the profile of the mission they actually fly.

2. For these reasons, including many types of aircraft will be opening a Pandora's box of wrangles between the two sides.

Should Shorter-Range TNF Systems Be Included

Discussion has concentrated, again arbitrarily, on TNF systems of over 1000 kilometers (or sometimes 1000 miles) in range. The arguments *for* including at least some shorter-range systems are

1. From NATO's perspective shorter-range Soviet systems based in Eastern Europe pose much the same threat as longer-range systems based well inside the Soviet Union. Witness, for example, SS–12 missiles with a range of 900 kilometers (or their successors, the SS–22s) based in Poland or Czechoslovakia, and SS–20s based east of the Urals. Both may look strategic to Western Europeans, and the Soviet view of shorter-range American systems no doubt is the obverse.

2. Politically, just as SALT II dramatized the SS–20 by excluding it, so LRTNF talks could underscore the threat posed by the shorter-range Soviet systems they left out. NATO could find it had solved its SS–20 problem only to have it replaced by an SS–21, SS–22 and SS–23 problem.

Yet the arguments *against* including shorter-range systems are formidable:

1. It would vastly complicate negotiations that aredy are overburdened. The talks would become negotiations over what was to be negotiated. It will be hard enough to compare SS–20s with GLCMs with Backfire bombers; adding shorter-range systems would only compound those problems of incommensurability.

2. As more short-range systems are included, the overall balance comes to be dominated by tactical aircraft whose status as threater-nuclear weapons clearly is more questionable than for longer-range systems. For example, of 3100 nuclear-capable Soviet aircraft, two-thirds have ranges of 750 kilometers or less.[7]

3. As a matter of negotiability, adding more short-range systems does not improve the balance from NATO's point of view, quite the contrary. For example, for all TNF systems over one hundred miles in range, the gross

Figure 7–4. Soviet Backfire Bomber

Warsaw Pact advantage in launchers is about three to one. If systems that seem clearly in the LRTNF category are excluded, the Warsaw Pact advantage rises to more than three to one. Moreover, the Soviet-American balance in shorter-range TNF is even more heavily tilted in the Soviet favor, since U.S. allies in Western Europe contribute relatively more to the balance than do the Soviet Warsaw Pact allies.

How to Treat Third-Country Nuclear Forces

There are two issues here. One is whether, and how, to include British and French nuclear forces in the LRTNF talks. The other is how to count Soviet LRTNF that is primarily oriented toward China but is mobile, or at least movable.

What to Do about British and French Forces

On this score the position of the two governments is firm and likely to remain so: their forces must be excluded. The justification—the forces are strategic in purposes, not theater—fronts for the real logic of exclusion—in both cases the forces are still small enough so that more than token reductions would render them meaningless. The Soviet position on British and French forces has moved back and forth over time. At times Soviet spokesmen have indicated that those forces could be excluded from the Geneva talks provided that they were included in future negotiations over central-strategic systems. However, more recent Soviet constructions of the LRTNF balance have included British and French forces. Soviet negotiators are virtually certain either to want to include British and French forces, or to want some compensation for them, a demand that runs back to the beginning of SALT I.[8] As those forces are modernized, it will be harder and harder for the United States to make the argument that they should be dismissed as part of the noise. On current plans, the French could have as many as 750 SLBM warheads, probably MIRVed, by the end of this decade. If the British proceed with the Trident program, they would have 512 MIRVed warheads on four boats by sometime in the 1990s.

This issue will have to be confronted at some point, but it need not block the negotiations early on; there are plenty of other issues to be sorted out first. The question of what to do about British and French forces would be easier to to handle in merged LRTNF–strategic negotiations, in which those forces would be relatively minor portions of the total balance.

How to Handle Soviet Forces Oriented toward China

Again, this is an old issue, with the Soviet Union long having insisted in SALT that it should be given some extra allowance because of its need to deal with Chinese nuclear forces. That issue will take specific form in the Geneva talks because about a third of the SS–20s are out of range of Western Europe and about a quarter of Soviet nuclear-capable aircraft are deployed facing China. But SS–20s can be moved, perhaps even by air, and aircraft could be rapidly deployed westward, so NATO will be as reluctant to exclude China-oriented systems as the Soviet Union will be to include them. Eventually it should be possible to handle that problem, at least for the SS–20s, with a combination of a global ceiling on all systems coupled with a subceiling on those based within range of Western Europe. It is worth noting, however, that all the Soviet proposals made thus far to freeze their LRTNF-missile deployments if NATO suspends its December 1979 decision have applied only to systems in European Russia—west of the Urals—and have thus excluded even the third of the SS–20s deployed in central Russia, able to target both Western Europe and China.[9]

How to Verify an LRTNF Agreement

Verification obviously will be a serious problem, for reasons that are familiar from SALT but worse in this case: most of the systems under discussion are mobile, many are small and thus easy to conceal, and there will be the need to distinguish between nuclear-capable and conventional versions of the same system in a way that can be verified. The central point is that verification will become more of a problem, and be more likely to hang up the negotiations, the more ambitious an agreement is sought. For example, the United States verifies the number of SS–20 launchers with satellite photography, much as with Soviet ICBMs. It does so by observing the activity at SS–20 bases, often without actually seeing an SS–20 launcher. That would provide tolerable verification of numbers of SS–20 launchers, but if agreements sought to constrain numbers of missiles with launchers, additional verification procedures probably would be required. Similarly, if agreements go beyond missiles to include aircraft it will be necessary to design ways, verifiable to the other side, to distinguish nuclear or nuclear-capable versions from those that are purely conventional. That will in any case be necessary for cruise missiles.

Soviet Approach

The Soviet approach to the issue is painfully plain. Brezhnev's interview in *Der Spiegel* in the fall of 1981 neatly summarized most of it. It begins with the strong assertion that East-West parity in LRTNF already exists. It is the NATO December 1979 decision, not the Soviet Union, that threatens to disrupt that happy state of affairs. What the United States seeks is yet another means of strategic attack on the Soviet Union. Worse, the new weapons (especially the Pershing IIs) are first-strike weapons. For the Western Europeans, Soviet pronouncements hold out both an inducement and a threat, more or less explicit: states that renounce nuclear weapons on their territory will be spared by the Soviet Union, but, since the new deployments are an American scheme to gain unilateral advantage over the Soviet Union, European states that accept them must bear the consequences.

For negotiating purposes, the Soviet position has changed little since Brezhnev's speech in East Berlin in October 1979: by Soviet lights, parity already exists, and so the Soviet Union will be prepared to reduce its own LRTNF, but only if NATO rescinds or suspends its December 1979 decisions. Moreover, the Soviets have continued to insist that the negotiations must be broadened beyond land-based missiles, to include FBS.

In February 1982, for example, the Soviet Union proposed that both sides reduce their INF (ranges over 1000 kilometers) to 600 by 1985 and to 300 by 1990.[10] Notice, however, that those reductions would apply to delivery systems, not warheads; to systems in Europe, thus excluding Soviet INF, which is deployed in central Russia or in the East but which is moveable; and to the INF balance as constituted by Brezhnev, which included Western aircraft while excluding comparable Soviet planes. That proposal also repeated the call for a freeze on new deployments while negotiations proceeded. The effect would be to prevent the new NATO deployments while protecting Soviet SS-20s.

The Soviet objective seems transparent: to forestall the deployment of the 572 American missiles. Tactically, Soviet leaders evidently are not yet convinced that they will actually have to pay a price in their own SS-20 deployments; they still seem to believe that the weight of nuclear opposition in Europe will itself bring down the December 1979 decision. By the end of 1982, however, the Soviet Union will have over 300 SS-20s deployed, well over the number originally assumed to be the target total. Thus, if need be, the Soviets easily could offer a twenty percent reduction in SS-20s in exchange for no NATO GLCMs and Pershings. It is predictable that they will play that card, but not before West European politics seems to require it, and their own SS-20 deployments to permit it.

Negotiating Alternatives for NATO

Obviously, combining different decisions about specific negotiating issues in different ways would produce a host of theoretical approaches to the negotiations. Yet, equally obviously, the future is more constrained than that. An agreement based on other than the principle of parity, for example, simply is not in the cards. NATO faces three broad negotiating alternatives, each with a number of possible variants.

A Quick Outcome

This category comprises two very different negotiating offers. One, seeking a quick agreement, would be limited in intent and scope. It would rest on the calculation that only an agreement would suffice to protect (some portion of) the 572 missiles from antinuclear opponents in Europe. It might be limited to modern, land-based long-range theater missiles, seeking to do little more than ratify the programs of the two sides. For example, a rough parity in launchers might be codified for 1985-1986; by that point NATO would be perhaps halfway through its deployment program, and the Soviet Union might also have about 250 launchers, provided it stopped the SS-20 program at its current state (and dismantled all the SS-4s and SS-5s) or provided NATO were still willing to exclude those deployed only in range of China.[11] A rough parity in warheads might exist at the end of the decade, if NATO deployed all its 572 missiles, the Soviet Union stopped the SS-20 at 250 and NATO was willing to exclude the China-oriented one-third of those. That parity might be extended, again crudely, to aircraft (156 American F–111s with two warheads each, against 135 Soviet Backfires with three or four each. By 1988 the Soviet Union might have some 375 total Backfires, with the half devoted to naval aviation and the quarter or so of the remaining based in the East excluded from the LRTNF agreement). Alternatively, aircraft might be deferred until later, with both sides agreeing not to circumvent the missile agreement through radical changes in patterns of aircraft deployment.[12]

Such an approach would be simpler to negotiate than other alternatives, though far from easy, and it is consistent with the tack NATO has taken until now. About strategic systems, it would make only the relatively modest assumptions that some constraints would remain—such as is the case currently with both the United States and the Soviet Union tacitly abiding by the qualitative limits in SALT II whose breach would be irrevocable under the terms of the treaty itself. On the other hand, the quick agreement would hardly be impressive as arms control. Nor would it necessarily be tempting to the Soviet Union if it only seemed to ratify NATO's deployment plans, even if NATO made an LRTNF agreement the price of admission to the strategic talks.

At the other extreme, NATO might seek a quick outcome by making an offer, along the lines of President Reagan's zero option—nondeployment of the 572 missiles in return for the dismantling of all SS–20s[13]—virtually on a take-it-or-leave-it basis.[14] It would mean holding firm even if, as is likely, the Soviet Union rejected the offer. Such an approach would rest on a number of assumptions. While there would still be military arguments for NATO to deploy some new systems even if no SS–20s existed—(these arguments are spelled out below)—this approach would presume that the political and psychological overhang in Western Europe produced by the SS–20s would justify abandoning NATO's deployment plans to eliminate it. It would also imply a calculation that NATO could take and hold the arms control high ground, even if the Soviet Union rebuffed a take-it-or-leave-it offer, thus permitting NATO to go ahead and deploy the 572 missiles. It would also tend to presume that, given the formidable problems with LRTNF negotiations, NATO should not venture far onto that terrain, ever, or at least until the strategic negotiations were well underway.

A Merged LRTNF-Strategic Negotiation

This would have the advantages mentioned earlier. Doctrinally, it would keep together systems that from the perspective of NATO's deterrent are similar. It would also make it easier to handle the existing imbalances in LRTNF by encompassing them in a broader balance. While it would open NATO to potentially awkward Soviet offers targeted where European and American interests seemed to diverge, the other side of that coin could have advantages for European interests and for Alliance cohesion. It would force the United States to be explicit in addressing trade-offs between central and European-based systems.

The principle disadvantage is that it would tie the LRTNF negotiations to strategic talks whose future is cloudy. The merged negotiations, even once underway, would be immensely complicated. Under the best of circumstances an agreement would take years, not months or even tens of months. That simply may not do given the pressures of European politics. Such a negotiation could also increase the chances that the focus of concern would shift to uncovered shorter-range TNF systems. That would suggest the need at least for some sort of interim freeze on shorter-range systems while the LRTNF-strategic negotiations proceeded; that in turn would complicate the discussions still further.

A Comprehensive TNF Negotiation

A negotiation that sought to deal with all nuclear weapons, from strategic through short-range, clearly would be a recipe for accomplishing nothing. There simply would be too many incommensurable systems, too many asymmetries in force posture and doctrine. A negotiation that dealt with all TNF, from the SS–20 down to, but excluding, only so-called battlefield-nuclear weapons with ranges less than, say, 100 miles still would be bafflingly complicated. Yet it might be conceivable in a way that a negotiation also comprising strategic weapons would not.

Such a comprehensive TNF negotiation would rest on two calculations, one technical, the other political. Technically, since any division of TNF systems, especially one based on range, is essentially arbitrary, it is better to face that fact directly and let the negotiations capture a broad range of weapons. (Of course, the point at which weapons were classified as battlefield would itself be somewhat arbitrary. Still, there does seem to be a significant difference between weapons designed to influence the course of the immediate battle and those that can strike deeper into enemy formations.) These comprehensive TNF negotiations would also provide NATO an opportunity, and perhaps an incentive, to trade away shorter-range systems for the longer, thus reducing the current preponderance of short-range—and, in my view, essentially worthless—systems in its nuclear arsenal.[15]

Politically, comprehensive TNF negotiations would seek to anticipate the next nuclear issue. Negotiations limited to LRTNF could easily dramatize the threat posed by shorter-range weapons, which were excluded for reasons described earlier. The Soviet Union has three new shorter-range missile systems, the SS–21, SS–22 and SS–23, ready for deployment with its forces in

Eastern Europe. Each of these systems has longer range, more accuracy, and perhaps more mobility than the weapon it will replace (FROG, Scaleboard, and Scud, respectively). Without constraints on shorter-range systems, Soviet leaders could manipulate the pace of SS–21, SS–22 and SS–23 deployments to produce much the same anxiety about the credibility of NATO's deterrent as that brought about by the SS–20, and for much the same reason. Including shorter-range systems in the negotiations would anticipate that problem.

Yet the difficulties with comprehensive TNF negotiations are awesome. Most have been mentioned earlier: the sheer complexity would be boggling; shorter-range systems dominate longer-range TNF in numbers to an extent that may reflect neither the military threat they pose, nor their political significance; adding shorter-range systems does not diminish the numerical imbalance in the Soviet favor, but rather increases it, thus making it all the harder to conjure a negotiated parity as the result.

Moreover, the notion that comprehensive TNF negotiations might force NATO toward more clarity in its thinking about TNF is fraught with risks.[16] In that regard, the Mutual and Balanced Force Reduction (MBFR) talks in Vienna constitute a mixed precedent. The NATO allies have managed an impressive degree of unity over a long period of time, and the process does seem in many respects to have produced a clearer and more shared understanding of the military balance and the role of arms control instruments (so-called associated or confidence-building measures, for example). However, in other respects the MBFR negotiations have distorted NATO force planning; nuclear-capable F–4s were retained in Europe for longer than made military sense because NATO did not want to gut its offer to reduce them as part of an MBFR agreement. And whatever insights about the military balance in Central Europe may have been developed within allied governments, they have not had much effect on the public discussion; on the contrary, the MBFR focus on numbers seems to have reinforced the common misperception of NATO's hopeless inferiority on the central front. NATO badly needs to be clearer in thinking about the role of TNF; the beginning of greater clarity would be a force posture that relied less on short-range systems and a doctrine that depended less on the threat to use nuclear weapons first. Yet whether comprehensive TNF negotiations would advance or impede that process of clearing minds remains a question.

Other approaches are possible. None will suffice on its own, although several might be useful as complements to other approaches. For instance, now that SS–20 warheads number more than the total of LRTNF warheads NATO plans to deploy by 1988, the time is past when NATO might have tried tacit restraint, keying its own deployments to the pace of the SS–20. Seeking agreement with the Soviets to store LRTNF warheads separately from launchers, and out of range of the Soviet Union for NATO, and Western Europe for the Soviet Union, is a novel idea but probably impossible to verify.[17]

Other sorts of nuclear confidence-building measures may offer more promise, at least as complements to other agreements. For instance, the two sides might agree to deploy certain kinds of short-range TNF out of range of the other. That would pose awkward questions for NATO's first-use doctrine, but those questions are, in my view, long overdue.

Negotiating Approaches and Objectives

The central danger of the LRTNF talks is that NATO has drifted into them for purely political reasons, with little sense of what objective they might serve. NATO is committed to a process without much idea where it wants that process to lead. In part that is true because the experts have given the politicians so little help; they have added arcane tangles to an issue that is complicated and ambiguous enough already. Their guidance about negotiations has amounted to little more than "don't do it." It is thus left to the politicians to slice through the tangle that analysts have bequested. Yet there is real danger that the slicing will be based purely on immediate political calculations, and thus will hurt military interests or even fail to serve the intended long-term political purposes, or both.

What should be clear is that different objectives suggest different negotiating approaches. If the principal objective is getting NATO out of the LRTNF-negotiating business, at least for the time being, while limiting damage to Alliance politics and to the chances of deploying the 572 missiles, that suggests a take-it-or-leave-it offer that seeks the arms control high ground—something like the zero option. If, by contrast, the main goal is trying to manage the political climate in Europe so that at least a portion of the 572 missiles will be deployed, such a take-it-or-leave-it offer will not, in my judgment, suffice. Under this object, NATO should pursue some version of the quick-agreement approach (even recognizing that no agreement would be all that quick). That would mean an aggressive pursuit of the LRTNF talks coupled with modest hopes about how many systems could be included, and a relatively loose link to the strategic negotiations.

Pursuing merged-LRTNF-strategic negotiations would give primacy to maintaining NATO's doctrinal link between those two categories of weapons. Politically, it would presume the value of better structured negotiations even if the price were considerable delay before any agreement could be reached. Finally, a comprehensive TNF negotiation would also imply that European politics could tolerate delay. It would suggest that the principal objective was avoiding the next set of nuclear problems in the Alliance, with a secondary goal being to force NATO toward a more realistic TNF posture and doctrine.

The face of the LRTNF issue is now dominated by politics, but in framing any negotiating approach it is imperative to keep in mind the military arguments that touched off the current episode. The first was that NATO's existing TNF posture is extremely vulnerable. That is particularly so for the longer-range systems: nuclear-capable aircraft are vulnerable on the ground, even on fifteen-minute alert, are more and more dubious in their ability to penetrate Soviet air defenses, and are badly needed for conventional roles in any event. Current missiles, such as the Pershing I, while mobile, are cumbersome and can only be fired from a limited number of presurveyed sites. The second argument blends military and political considerations, and is harder to state simply. Not only is NATO's existing LRTNF obsolescent, but there is little of it, leaving aside SLBMs. In the context of Soviet nuclear-force improvements across the entire range—from ICBMs, to the SS–20, to shorter-range missiles—that raises concern over gaps in NATO's spectrum of deterrence. This argument all too often slides into talk of missing "rungs" in "ladders of nuclear escalation," arcane and theological to people in the street, yet there is something to it. The point to notice is that the Soviet SS–20 is relevant to both arguments but decisive to neither. Existing NATO LRTNF would be vulnerable and dubious even without the SS–20, and while the growth of Soviet LRTNF, like the SS–20, is part of what occasioned the second concern, it is only part, and not the most important part at that. Strategic parity is more critical.

Hence NATO would need to modernize its TNF, especially at longer range, even if there were no SS–20s. That, in turn, means that some modernization options must be protected in any negotiating approach. The 572 missiles could be bargained away; so might all land-based LRTNF missiles. But that would make it all the more important to retain some sea-based options. Given Soviet concerns about cruise missiles, land and sea-based, treatment of those is likely to be a point of major contention in the negotiations.

Balancing political imperatives with military sense, or the need to negotiate seriously with realism about what might result will not be easy. There is, in the TNF issue, the potential for strain in NATO more serious than the multilateral-force (MLF) episode of the 1960s. In managing the issue, none of the negotiating alternatives is tempting. My own preference would be the active pursuit of a quick—and limited—agreement in the short run, while laying the basis for a tightly related, or even merged LRTNF-strategic negotiation over the long term. The zero option is not bad as a negotiating opener, at least it recognizes the need to take the arms-control high ground in ways that are not purely propaganda, to diminish the impression in Europe that the Soviet Union makes proposals and the West rejects them. Beyond openers, the immediate NATO objective would be to set a cap on the SS–20, preferably one that required significant reductions, while protecting NATO's right to some LRTNF modernization, even if not necessarily the 572 land-based missiles.

Notes

1. For more detailed background to the current negotiations, see Gregory F. Treverton, *Nuclear Weapons in Europe,* Adelphi Paper No. 168 (London: IISS, 1981).
2. His speech is printed in *Survival,* 20 no. 1 (January/February 1978).
3. NATO Communique, MC(79)22, December 12, 1979.
4. Brezhnev used these numbers in an interview in 1981 with the German magazine *Der Spiegel.* It is reproduced in English in Foreign Broadcast Information Service, Daily Report, Soviet Union, November 2, 1981, p. G8; and the relevant portions are excerpted in English in *The Guardian* (London), November 23, 1981. He disaggregated the Western figure in the original interview and provided additional information on the Soviet number during his visit to Bonn, reported in *The Times* (London), November 25, 1981.
5. This idea had been suggested earlier by some German and British analysts. For an intriguing proposal along those lines, see Lawrence Freedman, "The Dilemma of Theater Nuclear Arms Control," *Survival,* 23, no. 1 (January/February 1981): 2–10.
6. Christoph Bertram makes such an argument. See his "The Implications of Theater Nuclear Weapons in Europe," *Foreign Affairs,* 60, no. 2 (Winter 1981/1982), 323ff.
7. Calculated from *The Military Balance, 1981-82* (London: IISS, 1981), p. 128.
8. In Brezhnev's *Der Spiegel* interview cited in note 1, for example, he said of the British and French forces: "The Soviet Union is not pressing for the reduction of precisely those potentials. It is the overall result and the overall balance that is important to us."
9. See, for example, Brezhnev's report of the Central Committee to the 26th Congress of the Soviet Communist Party, February 23, 1981, excerpted in *Survival,* 23, no. 3 (May/June 1981): 134–137.
10. This proposal was mentioned by Brezhnev in early February 1982. See Foreign Broadcast Information Service, Daily Report, Soviet Union, February 3, 1982, p. AA1. For more detail, see the TASS article by Colonel General Nikolay Chervov, FBIS, Daily Report, Soviet Union, February 11, 1982, p. AA1.
11. This section draws on Freedman, "The Dilemma of Nuclear Arms Control."
12. Lynn Davis outlines a simple proposal along similar lines. See her "A Proposal for TNF Arms Control," *Survival,* 23, no. 6 (November/December 1981): 242–246.
13. President Reagan made the zero-option offer in a speech to the National Press Club in Washington, November 18, 1981.
14. A similar take-it-or-leave-it offer is suggested by William Hyland,

"Soviet Theater Forces and Arms Control Policy," *Survival,* 23, no. 5 (September/October 1981): 194–199.

15. This argument is coming to be widely shared. For my version, see my *Nuclear Weapons in Europe,* cited above, especially chapter III.

16. For a relatively sanguine argument on this score, see Michael Higgins and Christopher Makins, "European Theater Nuclear Forces and " 'Gray Area' Arms Control," Paper presented to the Sixth Annual National Security Affairs Conference, National Defense University, Washington, D.C., July 1979, pp. 23–25.

17. This idea was suggested by Alton Frye in his "How to Save SALT," *Foreign Policy* 39 (Summer 1980).

8 The Atlantic Alliance: Summing Up

Peter Corterier

In 1959, the then commander-in-chief of NATO in Europe, General Norstad, said that if you make observations that people are glad to hear you may be considered an authority; but if you make necessary but unpleasant observations you are branded as a thermonuclear hawk.

I start with this remark by General Norstad because it was made at a time when, as at present, nuclear weapons were being debated with a great degree of passion and idealism, but regrettably, in many cases, with little knowledge of the facts. Unlike the countries of the Eastern block, Western societies are marked by a frank discussion of all political issues that are of public interest. The attention of the media naturally focuses above all on the frequently very vociferous activities of minorities. Consequently, in Western countries the impression is often created that the activities of these minorities reflect the views of the vast majority of the population. Any politician who maintains contact with the public knows, even without opinion polls, that this impression is wrong.

What are—as General Norstad put it—the observations that are not gladly heard but are nonetheless necessary? The fundamental observation that continues to hold true for any security policy is that effective nuclear deterrence is vital for the preservation of peace. What, then, is the situation with regard to the effectiveness of deterrence in Europe? For over ten years the West sought to meet the Soviet challenge with a combination of defense capability and a readiness to cooperate with the Warsaw Pact. I cannot here describe in detail the tangible improvements and facilities that have been achieved by the treaties based on this policy for the people of my country, the Federal Republic of Germany, in particular. I need only mention the Quadripartite Agreement on Berlin and the Basic Treaty with the German Democratic Republic: hundreds of thousands of families separated by the wall and the barbed wire were, as a result of these treaties, at last able to meet again. Tens of thousands of people were finally able to leave the Soviet Union and Poland and join their relatives in the Federal Republic of Germany. Last but not least: the situation in and around Berlin is largely free from tension.

Arms control efforts are also part of this realistic policy of detente, which was designed to achieve an accommodation with the Soviet Union, at least in individual sectors. A limited amount of success, which should not be

---

(Speech given to the Arms Control Association Conference in Brussels September 21, 1981)

underrated, was indeed attained, for instance, with regard to strategic weapons. Unfortunately, it has not been possible to induce the Soviet Union to limit the massive buildup of its conventional and medium-range nuclear weapons or renounce its power-political advances in parts of the Third World and exercise restraint. Particularly conspicuous are the efforts undertaken by Moscow since 1977 to modernize and expand its medium-range nuclear capability targeted on Europe. This development occurred more or less in the shadow of the SALT negotiations. The Soviet Union managed to gain acceptance of parity in intercontinental systems, but at the same time enlarged its LRTNF superiority by putting into operation a completely new generation of weapons (the SS–20 missiles and Backfire bombers).

This then, is the situation with which the alliance was confronted. The Soviet Union did not react to the concern expressed in this context by the West and by my government in particular from 1977 onwards. The Soviet Union must face the charge of ignoring one of the rules of fundamental importance for stability in this nuclear age. The proposals for negotiations that it floated shortly before the NATO two-track decision were obviously designed to split the alliance and gave no indication of Soviet willingness to reduce its superiority to any substantial extent. Thus the prime purpose of the demand for modernization of the alliance's LRTNF capability, as contained in the two-track decision, is to reduce the disparity that has emerged.

After outlining the military *raison d'etre* of the two-tracked decision, I should now like to deal with its arms-control aspects. Unlike the East, the West did not simply initiate the production of medium-range weapons and confront the other side with a *fait accompli*. Instead, for the first time in military history, it combined a decision on weapons modernization from the outset with a proposition for arms control. This twofold nature of the decision is based on the alliance strategy set out in the Harmel Report of 1967, in other words, on a fundamental conviction formulated by the Western Alliance no fewer than fourteen years previously. According to the report, the dual objective of the Alliance is—through both a capacity for defense and a readiness for detente—to strengthen European security, broaden the basis for cooperation between East and West, and seek ways and means of reducing, or at least defusing, existing potential for conflict. This approach rests on the realization that weapons alone cannot guarantee security and that arms efforts must therefore be incorporated into an overall strategy.

To us, defense efforts and arms control are equal, necessary and complementary components of a realistic security policy. We are fully aware that arms control cannot replace defense. Hence, we fully concur with Alexander Haig who stated the following in his keynote speech on arms-control policy before the Foreign Policy Association in New York on July 14, 1981: "Our first principle is that our arms control efforts will be an instrument of, not a replacement for, a coherent allied security policy."

Both defense and arms control efforts must be geared to the principle of military equilibrium. Just as we cannot ensure our freedom in a state of military inferiority, security cannot be guaranteed in the long run by seeking military superiority. In the final analysis, our own security always presupposes security on the other side as well. Striving for superiority on our part would, without doubt, prompt the Soviet Union to try to draw level at all costs. This jointly fueled arms race would result in permanent instability at an ever higher level of arms, in other words an uncurbed growth of potential for threats and conflict.

We are, of course, fully aware that, in spite of the Soviet Union's repeated verbal acknowledgment of the principle of military equilibrium, constant efforts are needed to preserve the balance between East and West, or redress it where it has been upset.

Permit me now to look at another important aspect of our arms control concept. This is the linkage of arms control with the Soviet Union's conduct in foreign policy and defense matters. We agree with the view expressed by former Secretary Haig in the speech I just cited that the various instruments of foreign and defense policy cannot be separated from one another. It would be an inherent contradiction to accept Soviet agression for the sake of maintaining arms control.

On the other hand, we must rid ourselves of the notion that arms control is merely a device for granting or withholding benefits as a means of rewarding or punishing the Soviet Union for its conduct. In other words, arms control is, like any other instrument of our foreign or defense policies, not an end in itself. It has a high intrinsic value that must also be taken into consideration. Individual situations need to be examined to be sure that withholding these benefits from the other side does not, in terms of the overall balance of advantages and disadvantages, actually adversely affect one's own side.

The developments so far show that the parallel approach of the two-track decision is the right one:

The NATO modernization program is being implemented as planned.

The Soviet Union, realizing that modifications of this program can only be attained through negotiation, has, contrary to its initial reaction, accepted the Western offer for negotiations.

The alliance ought to examine whether this successful parallel approach would not be expedient in other areas, too. The United States has quite rightly made it clear that its security efforts are not directed solely toward strengthening its military capabilities, but also, with equal seriousness, toward the pursuit of bilateral and multilateral arms control. Thus, parallel to its defense efforts, the Alliance must continue to follow the political goal of integrating the Soviet Union, in the long run, into a system of limitations established through treaties, and thus bring about greater stability. Our common responsibility for peace requires this of us.

After examining the military and arms control aspects of the two-track decision, I should now like to deal in some detail with a subject which is a particular concern of mine and is of decisive importance for the issues covered in this book: I am referring to the transatlantic relationship, and the relations between our two countries in particular. The Federal Minister for Foreign Affairs, Herr Genscher, stated the following in the Bundestag on September 10, 1981:

> Our policy rests on the firm foundation of our friendship with the United States. Our two countries constitute a community of fate which is founded on shared security interests and is firmly embedded in the shared values of freedom, a democratic way of life, self-determination and human rights. This German-American partnership is a decisive factor for international stability and the security of the West into which the Federal Republic of Germany has been irrevocably integrated.

According to various opinion polls conducted recently on the subject of NATO and security, even more people in the Federal Republic of Germany are now in favor of close relations with the United States than was the case twenty-five years ago.

By virtue of this firmly rooted partnership, we are able, and are indeed obliged, to discuss with one another common problems and concerns in a frank and friendly manner. We all know—at least the newspapers say so—that different moods now prevail among the publics in our two countries. After a period of uncertainty, the United States has now again become aware of its strength and its traditional virtues. This is accompanied by the feeling that the detente of the 1970s yielded benefits for the Soviet Union alone. The Soviet invasion of Afghanistan is seen as a manifestation of this development.

In my country the situation is different: the *Ostpolitik* pursued by the government under Willy Brandt and the accompanying treaties led to tangible improvements, as I already outlined, for the German people, who are affected most by the confrontation with the Soviet power bloc in Europe.

The Soviet propaganda campaign against the NATO two-track decision has now aroused concern among Germans that Germany could again become a center of crisis as in the 1950s, and that they are in danger of losing the precious security gains and improved human contacts as a result of greater confrontation between the superpowers. These different political moods existing on either side of the Atlantic can lead to misconceptions and an incomplete view of the partner's aims. Thus, critical sections of the population of the Federal Republic express the fear that the United States is at present placing too much emphasis on military and economic might, while forgetting the Third World and not making sufficient use of the political and intellectual strength of the Atlantic Alliance.

I do not consider this form of concern justified. It is a typically shortsighted view of American intentions. In Alexander Haig's address to the American Bar Association in New Orleans on August 11, 1981, after referring to two outstanding elements of the American national character—idealism and pragmatism—he went on to say, "We have discovered that foreign policy, like law, must be rooted in the strength of our national character. A foreign policy that forsakes ideals in order to manipulate interests offends our sense of right. A foreign policy that forsakes power in order to pursue pieties offends our sense of reality. Only a vision with worthy ideals can capture our imagination. Only a practical program for achieving those ideals can be worthy of our support."

I feel that this true portrayal of the basic principles of U.S. foreign policy speaks for itself. Thus, the American government frequently refers to the concept of strength at present, because it wants to recover lost ground and not because it has succumbed to a fixation.

There are, however, also misconceptions on the other side. The growing concern over the arms race is shared by a great variety of groups in Europe and is not simply a symptom of pacifism. It would be specious to believe that only crypto-Communists or accomplices of the Kremlin are involved—Europeans have a different view of history from Americans. After losing their superiority in various wars, they now seek alternatives to a policy based solely on strength. I feel this aptly describes the deeper reasons for the concern in Europe over the international situation.

To make three final remarks on what I have just described:

There are, in my opinion, certain different lines of emphasis on either side of the Atlantic, but there is certainly not a transatlantic crisis.

It is imperative that we discuss, with greater frankness and trust than hitherto, any differences of opinion that arise, or, as President Reagan aptly has said, we should talk to one another more instead of talking about each other.

We must seek to ensure that we devote equal attention at all times to the two fundamental elements underlying the alliance—the necessary strength for self-defense and the moral consensus of member States.

Under these conditions, I am sure that, in view of the existing wealth of solidarity and affection for America, the vast majority of people in my country will continue to support any decisions on security that the alliance has to take.

Finally, I wish to express my confidence that the Alliance will succeed in coping with the problems facing us in this decade; I am convinced that the interplay of the great moral, intellectual, and material resources of North America and Western Europe affords an excellent guarantee for this.

NATO and Nuclear Deterrence

Richard Burt

NATO's decision of December 1979 to deploy long-range cruise and ballistic missiles in Europe and to pursue an arms control negotiation with the USSR concerning intermediate-nuclear forces (INF) have stimulated a debate that now transcends the military and political rationale upon which that decision was based. At issue are not comparative range, accuracy, and mobility of U.S. and Soviet systems; the proper components of a Eurostrategic balance; or the comparative advantage of sea-air, land-based systems. Many who challenge the decision of December 1979 do so, not on the grounds that there are better means of linking the U.S. strategic deterrent to Europe, but because they believe that Europe's security should not depend on nuclear deterrence of any type. To such fundamental objections, it avails little to argue the merits of ground-launched cruise missiles over sea-and air-launched cruise missiles, or to explain why it makes sense to replace the Pershing I with the Pershing II. To counter such objections, one must begin with a vision of Europe and of Europe's place in the world.

The View from Moscow

The Soviet Union sees Western Europe as an appendage of the two superpowers. Europe is relegated to a second-class status, its security a dependent function of the Soviet Union's. East Europeans may be forced to accept such discrimination, but certainly we in the West are not.

This anti-European vision of Europe is expressed in myriad ways. Soviet commentators tell us that the new U.S. Pershing missile represents an unacceptable threat to the Soviet Union because it would provide the Soviet Union only a five-minute warning of an attack. Yet what warning time of a comparable Soviet nuclear attack does Western Europe have? Thirty seconds perhaps.

The same sort of patronizing attitude is inherent in the Soviet concept of

---

An address by Richard Burt, director of the Bureau of Politico-Military Affairs, before the Arms Control Association Conference in Brussels, Belgium, September 23, 1981. Mr. Burt's speech was made a few weeks before the opening of Geneva INF negotiations, when U.S. policy was in the final stages of formulation and before President Reagan's November 18, 1981, zero-option speech.

forward-based systems. Somehow this term, even in Western parlance, refers only to American forces. It is never taken to mean Soviet missile and air forces massed in East Germany, Poland, Hungary, or Czechoslovakia, that threaten Western Europe. In other words, the American military presence in Western Europe is depicted as an unnatural historical aberration while the Soviet military hegemony over Eastern Europe and its preoccupation with West European security policies is viewed as a natural Soviet right.

The Soviet Union thus presumes that Western Europe should have more sympathy for problems of Soviet security than the Soviet Union does for that of Western Europe. And, remarkably, often we on both sides of the Atlantic do. For frequently we do not dismiss these self-serving Soviet propositions with the derision they deserve. On the contrary, we elevate them to the status of intellectually respectable arguments, and give them serious consideration in our domestic debates.

That the Soviet Union should put forward such propositions is evidence of how the Soviet Union treats its allies, and how it thinks about Western Europe. That anyone in the West finds merit in them is evidence that the Soviets have begun to affect how we think of ourselves.

Nothing more graphically illustrates the Soviet Union's vision of Europe than their position on theater-nuclear-arms control. For a decade the Soviet Union insisted that U.S. forces in Western Europe should be counted in the Strategic Arms Limitations Talks (SALT), but not Soviet forces in Eastern Europe. Only when confronted by the alliance's INF decision of 1979 were the Soviets forced, by NATO's cohesion and resolve, to fall back from this position, only to adopt a new series of equally patronizing proposals.

In 1979 the Soviets claimed a nuclear balance existed in Europe—but they kept deploying SS–20 missiles targeted against Western Europe. In 1980 the Soviets again said a balance existed and offered a moratorium on new missiles—but they kept deploying SS–20s. In 1981 the Soviets once again claimed a balance exists. They again offer a moratorium—but they still keep deploying SS–20s.

If any one of these Soviet statements regarding an existing balance were correct, the other two would, by definition, have to be wrong, for the West has deployed no new missiles since 1979, while the Soviets have, during this same period, deployed over 500 SS–20 warheads, not to speak of significant numbers of other new missile and nuclear-capable aircraft now targeted on Europe.

In fact, none of the three Soviet claims was true. Few in the West have ever thought they were. The Soviet technique in this instance is, however, more subtle than just their traditional resort to misinformation and deception, for, in offering a moratorium at widely disparate levels, the Soviet Union is really asserting that it has a right to nuclear, as well as conventional, superiority in Europe. The Soviet Union is insisting that Western Europe does not have a right to call upon American strength to counterbalance Soviet power and geographical advantage. This is the message behind the moratorium. Like other forms of subliminal advertising, it takes root slowly and imperceptibly.

More remarkable yet, the Soviet Union has attempted to attribute to the United States a view of Europe that is its own. The Soviet Union, in training, in doctrine, and in the structure of its forces, is prepared to fight a nuclear war in Europe. I am not suggesting that the Soviets intend to provoke a war, but if a war comes, the Soviets are ready to escalate rapidly to the nuclear level. They have trained and equipped their forces to prevail in such an environment. And they have structured and positioned their forces to limit the conflict to territory outside the USSR.

The United States, on the other hand, has for thirty years linked its fate with that of its European allies. In 1979 the United States responded positively to the desire of those allies to deploy, in Europe, new systems that could reach deep into the Soviet Union, in order to demonstrate that the USSR could not devastate Europe from a Russian sanctuary—that attack anywhere in Europe would result in unacceptable damage to the USSR itself.

The United States took this step in the full knowledge that the Soviet Union would most likely respond to an attack on its homeland by U.S. systems in Europe with an attack on the United States. Thus the emplacement of long-range U.S. cruise and ballistic missiles in Europe makes escalation of any nuclear war in Europe to an intercontinental exchange even more likely. This is why our allies asked for such a deployment. This is why the United States accepted. This is why the deployment strengthens deterrence.

Nevertheless, the INF decision is one of the most controversial security issues to have gripped the nations of the Alliance. On reflection, this should not be surprising: nuclear weapons raise profound moral, political, and strategic problems that must concern thoughtful people in healthy democracies. But in my view the INF debate also clearly demonstrates that we in the West are in danger of losing sight of our vision—the Western vision—of European security. Governments on both sides of the Atlantic have not sufficiently explained to new generations of Americans and Europeans how the Atlantic Alliance continues to offer a vision of Europe consistent with its security needs and its political values.

The Atlantic Vision

Throughout modern history, Europe has been the battleground where mankind's most intense, extended, and destructive conflicts have been waged. Twice in this century, war has devastated the continent, leaving fifty-million Europeans dead. Yet, since 1945, despite the proximity of a heavily armed hostile power, Europe has enjoyed a period of peace and prosperity unparalleled in the experience of mankind. How was peace secured? How has it been maintained?

By the middle of the twentieth century the ever-quickening pace of European warfare was brought to a halt by two innovations in Western strategic thought—collective defense and nuclear deterrence. In those early postwar years, the nations of Western Europe, along with the United States and Canada, formed an alliance based upon the principle that a threat to one was a threat to all. The objective of their alliance was purely defensive. Their strategy was one of deterrence. These nations sought to work together to minimize the risk of war by maximizing the risk to any potential aggressor of engaging in war. In particular, the United States, the strongest member of the new Alliance, proclaimed that it would regard an attack on its European allies as an attack on itself, and it committed its full military power to deter such an attack. This commitment remains today the foundation of American defense and foreign policy and the cornerstone of European security.

NATO's Three Pillars

NATO is an alliance of nations separated by 3,000 miles of ocean. The geopolitical situation of each ally is in some way unique; the threat it faces in some way different. Adversary forces are deployed throughout an area bordering directly on NATO's most populous, developed, and vulnerable regions. Geography thus provides the Warsaw Pact significant advantages. The Soviet Union can project military force in central Europe more easily and more quickly than can the United States. In consequence, it has been difficult for NATO—throughout its history—to provide a major conventional force sufficient in itself to insure its defense.

In order to defend this wide expanse of territory and to deter aggression against it at any point, NATO has come to rely on strategy based on three interrelated types of forces. At one end of the spectrum are NATO's conventional forces. The role of these forces is to meet any aggression at the level it occurs, and, if possible, to force the enemy to cease its aggression and withdraw. At the other end of the spectrum are America's intercontinental-range nuclear forces, which represent the ultimate guarantee of Western security. Between the two are the alliance's nuclear weapons deployed in Europe, which link NATO's conventional forces and the intercontinental-range systems based on U.S. soil. The presence of these nuclear systems in Europe insures that the deterrent value of America's strategic forces fully underwrites the defense of Europe. They underscore to a potential aggressor that there are no circumstances in which it could gain a victory over NATO's conventional forces without risking nuclear escalation.

The development of this strategy was not without difficulty for the alliance. In the 1950s, with the nightmare of the 1939–1945 war fresh in people's minds, there was less concern about lowering the nuclear threshold and a greater willingness to accept the risk of a nuclear exchange in order to keep the conventional threshold as high as possible. Thus early attempts to bolster conventional defense in Europe met with resistance from those who feared that those efforts meant that the United States no longer wished to shoulder the responsibilities of the nuclear umbrella. As Soviet nuclear capabilities grew, however, concern shifted to also encompass the now more familiar worry that moves to strengthen NATO's intermediate-nuclear capabilities have, as their ulterior motive, the confinement of any nuclear war to European territory.

These conflicting concerns led to the development, in the early 1960s, of NATO's strategy of flexible response. This strategy tied U.S. strategic forces firmly into a seamless web of conventional, intermediate-nuclear, and strategic-nuclear forces. The concept that underlies the strategy of flexible response is that neither Western Europe nor the United States must bear all the burdens or run all the risks of deterring war—everyone must do his part. The purpose of building up conventional and nuclear forces in Europe in the 1960s was not to supplant the deterrent role of U.S. strategic forces but to make their use in major conflict appear more credible, thus improving overall deterrence.

But NATO's flexible-response strategy was challenged at its inception when the Soviet Union, in the early 1960s, began to deploy large numbers of intermediate-range ballistic missiles (IRBMs)—SS-4s and SS-5s—as well as a formidable force of frontal aviation, all of which were designed to target Western Europe. The motive for this Soviet buildup was almost certainly political as well as military. Just as NATO's intermediate nuclear systems were designed to link Europe more closely with America's strategic arsenal, so Soviet systems targeted on Europe were meant to break that link, to isolate Europe, to threaten it from a Russian sanctuary that Europe could not, in turn, put at risk, and so to hold Europe a nuclear hostage.

The expansion of the Soviet IRBM force, coupled with Moscow's advantage in conventional forces, brought to reality a prospect that Europe had long faced—the possibility that a nuclear conflict might be limited to Europe. For over a decade, however, this threat was successfully met, not by an expansion of U.S. nuclear forces in Europe, but by an increase in the U.S. strategic arsenal in the 1960s, along with the development of British and French nuclear systems. During this period and into the 1970s, American strategic superiority provided the margin of security that permitted shortfalls in other areas of NATO's force structure.

The Changing Strategic Environment

The Soviet buildup has now continued for more than a decade beyond the end of the U.S. strategic buildup of the 1960s. It has continued through a period when the West pursued policies of detente, when the United States cut its military budgets, and when NATO undertook virtually no nuclear-force modernization. These Soviet actions have had a direct impact on the alliance's ability to implement its deterrent strategy of flexible response.

Soviet-force improvements have occurred at all levels and in all areas. Major improvements have occurred in the conventional forces facing Europe, the Far East, and the oil-rich regions of southwest Asia. Major improvements have occurred in Soviet airborne and seaborne forces capable of projecting Soviet power into regions further afield. Major improvements have also occurred in Soviet intercontinental nuclear forces and nuclear forces targeted on Europe. In this latter area, the Soviets have developed and are rapidly deploying new generations of short-range, medium-range, and long-range nuclear missiles, as well as several new types of nuclear-capable aircraft.

Thus, at the conventional level, the Soviet Union threatens Europe directly, through its local superiority in numbers and increasingly modernized forces, as well as indirectly, through its ability to project force into other regions of vital interest to Europe, such as the Persian Gulf. The growth in the Soviet conventional threat places a heavier burden on NATO's nuclear deterrent to keep the peace. Yet, at the same time the Soviet Union has achieved parity in intercontinental-range nuclear forces, it has moved into a position of clear superiority in those nuclear forces deployed in or targeted on Europe. In consequence, NATO's deterrent is being eroded at a time when the need for it is being heightened.

Although the Soviets over the last decade have enhanced their military capabilities across the board, they have given a high priority to the buildup of their intermediate nuclear forces threatening Europe. The deployment of the multiple independently-targetable reentry vehicle (MIRV) mobile SS–20 gives the Soviet Union a capability to hit, accurately and in great number, targets located anywhere in Western Europe from locations deep within the Soviet Union, far beyond the range of any of NATO's European-based systems. In the spring of 1981, West German Chancellor Schmidt wrote that the introduction of the SS–20 "has upset the military balance in Europe and created for itself an instrument of political pressure on the countries within the range of the SS–20, for which the West so far has no counterbalance."[1]

Today, SS–20 missiles are still being deployed in ever-increasing numbers. There are currently 250 SS–20 missiles deployed, carrying 750 warheads, along with 350 SS–4 and SS–5 missiles, for a total of 1,100 long-range missile warheads. At the same time, the Soviets have undertaken a comprehensive program of improvement and modernization of short- and medium-range missile forces threatening Europe, including the SS–21, SS–22, and SS–23, and of new aircraft with nuclear capability and missions, such as the Backfire, Fencer, Flogger, and Fitter.

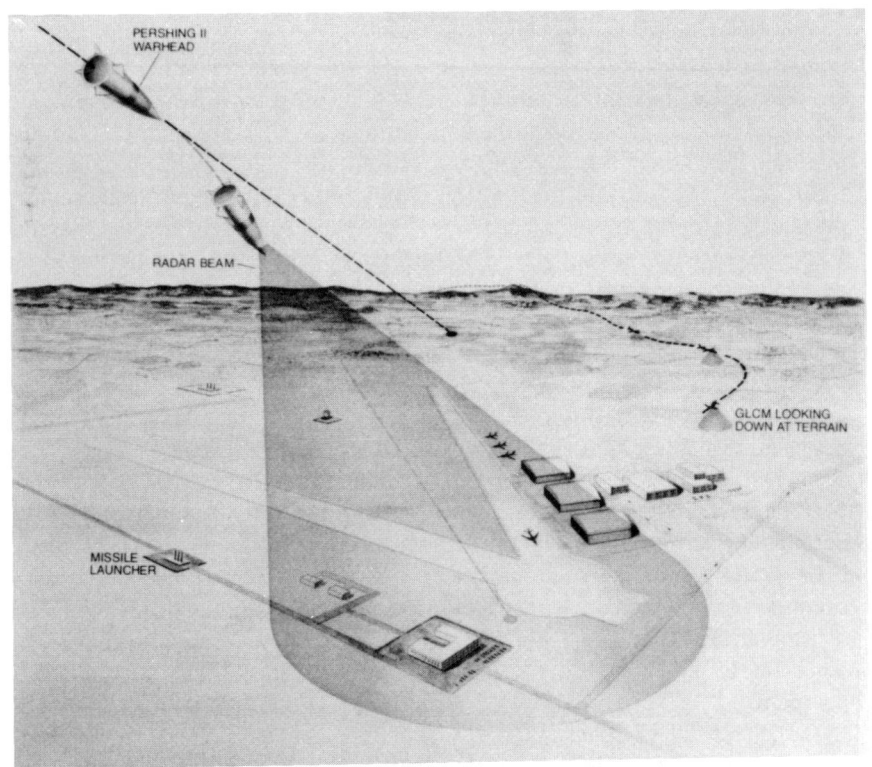

Figure 9–1. Pershing II and GLCM
Source: Kevin N. Lewis, "Intermediate-Range Nuclear Weapons," *Scientific American*, December 1980, p. 2.
Note: Hypothetical Attack by U.S. intermediate-range nuclear weapons on an airfield in Eastern Europe is depicted in this idealized scene. Both the Pershing II and the GLCM are distinguished not only by their extended range but also by their greatly improved accuracy compared with current NATO systems. The reentry vehicle of the Pershing II, which carries the nuclear warhead, is terminally guided by a radar-based area-correlation technique that compares the live radar return from the target area with a stored radar image of the area. Continual automatic comparisons of the two images generate control signals to maneuver the reentry vehicle, bringing it in with pinpoint accuracy on the assigned target. (The accuracy of the terminal-guidance system is independent of the range.) The reentry vehicle is too small and travels too fast for it to be shot down by current air defenses. The GLCM is equipped with an advanced terrain-contour-matching guidance system (called TERCOM), which is capable of directing the missile over a circuitous flight path to the target. The TERCOM system employs a radar altimeter to measure the altitude of the terrain along preselected segments of the route. The information from the altimeter is compared with stored data to signal appropriate changes in course and altitude. Here the GLCM is approaching the target area from the rear in order to avoid local air defenses. GLCM is designed to fly low, in effect hiding in the terrain.

NATO's Response

The comprehensive nature of the growing Soviet threat requires a comparably comprehensive NATO response in order to sustain NATO's deterrent strategy and so maintain a stable peace. NATO must improve its capability to meet and defeat aggression at the conventional level. To do so, NATO must maintain and, where possible, increase current force levels while regaining its traditional superiority in the quality of its military equipment, training, and morale of its forces with which the West has hitherto compensated for Warsaw Pact conventional advantages. The nuclear threshold will not be raised by degrading the capability of nuclear forces. Unfortunately those who seem to worry most about lowering the nuclear threshold seem among those least inclined to support the conventional modernization needed to raise it.

Yet improving NATO's conventional posture is not enough. For NATO to maintain the credibility of its deterrent strategy, it must shore up the link between the intercontinental and European-based nuclear systems. The Soviet Union must never be allowed to assume that there exists any level of conflict at which it could conclude hostilities victoriously, or that it can limit a conflict to Europe. In particular, the Soviet Union must never be permitted to believe that, under any circumstances, Soviet territory could serve as a sanctuary from which nuclear strikes in Europe could be launched without fear of retaliation in kind. To allow even the perception of such a gap in the deterrent to emerge would offer fresh opportunities for Soviet political coercion.

The steps NATO has taken to sustain its deterrent strategy include U.S. and allied conventional-force improvement, now underway, and a deployment in the United States of a more survivable intercontinental-missile system designed to reduce the growing vulnerability of the existing U.S. land-based missile force. An equally critical step in sustaining deterrence was the alliance's decision of December 1979 to modernize its long-range nuclear forces by deployment of 464 ground-launched cruise missiles and the replacement of 108 Pershing ballistic missiles with a model of greater range.

This decision to modernize NATO's long-range nuclear forces was a particularly important part of the overall NATO response to the Soviet buildup. The new systems will be mobile, and they will disperse in times of crisis, thus enhancing the survivability of NATO nuclear forces and reducing the dangers of a Soviet preemptive attack. The very existence of NATO's nuclear forces compels any aggressor to disperse its forces more widely and adopt less efficient modes of conventional attack, even at the early stages of any conflict. These new systems can also reach into the Soviet Union; thus their deployment to Europe will reinforce the Soviet leadership's realization that Soviet territory cannot be a sanctuary in wars from which long-range missiles like the SS–20, or aircraft such as the Backfire, could threaten

Western Europe with nuclear destruction. Finally, these systems, will be based in a number of member countries. They thus demonstrate the concept of shared risk, shared effort, and shared security upon which the Western Alliance is based.

When INF modernization is seen in this broader context of Western deterrence strategy, the myths that have come to surround the Alliance decision of December 1979 melt away.

The deployment of long-range cruise and ballistic missiles to Europe does not move NATO away from its existing strategy of flexible response. Rather, the INF decision is essential to sustaining NATO strategy. In particular, this deployment will link more firmly the alliance's existing nuclear forces in Europe to the U.S. strategic deterrent.

This deployment was not thrust by the United States upon the Europeans. Rather it represents a considered American response to a widely felt European need for an evolutionary adjustment of NATO's capabilities to take account of the onset of strategic parity and the massive and continuing buildup of Soviet theater forces, such as the SS–20.

The deployment does not give the alliance a qualitatively new capability. The United States has had systems in Europe capable of striking the Soviet Union since 1952. This new deployment will permit NATO to retain that capability and retain that element of our deterrent strategy, despite improvements in Soviet air defense, the aging of our own systems, an increasing need to commit NATO's aircraft resources to conventional roles, and large-scale new deployments of Soviet INF.

This deployment does not increase the alliance's reliance on nuclear weapons. Rather, in providing NATO a more balanced intermediate-nuclear force, this planned deployment has already permitted a significant net reduction in older and more vulnerable nuclear weapons located in Europe.

This deployment does not represent a step toward the development of a NATO nuclear-war–fighting capability. It is the Soviet Union that is developing the capability to fight and win a nuclear war in Europe. This deployment will force on them the realization that NATO will not fight a war on their terms, will not permit them to regionalize a conflict to exclude their territory, and will not permit them to hold Europe a nuclear hostage.

Theater-Nuclear-Arms Control

The 1979 INF decision not only promises enhanced prospects for deterrence of war in Europe, it also holds out the prospect of a serious effort to negotiate reductions in U.S. and Soviet intermediate-nuclear forces. As a result of NATO demonstrating the resolve to modernize its INF, the USSR has been persuaded to put on the negotiating table, for the first time, nuclear forces that threaten the allies. Without modernization there would be no prospect of limiting the Soviet nuclear threat to Europe.

I take no credit for noting that Florence Nightingale's injunction regarding hospitals—that their first task was to avoid spreading disease—applied equally to arms control. An arms controller's first imperative is to limit arms in ways that do not make wars more likely. The Reagan administration believes that if arms control is to reinforce the prospects for peace, it must be closely integrated with defense and foreign policies of its practitioners.

The United States is committed to making arms control a coherent, supportive part of its total national-security program. We recognize that arms control, properly pursued, helps to reduce the threat we face and contributes to stability and peace.

In July 1981, Secretary of State Haig outlined the principles that will guide the United States as it enters into theater-nuclear-arms control as well as other arms control talks:

> Arms control will be an instrument of, not a replacement for, a coherent Alliance security policy.
>
> We will seek balanced arms control agreements.
>
> Arms control must include effective means of verification and mechanisms for security compliance.
>
> Our strategy must consider the totality of various arms control processes, not only those that are being specifically negotiated.
>
> We will demonstrate our seriousness by insisting that whatever the scope of negotiations, we are prepared to accept reductions to the lowest possible level based on equal, balanced limits on comparable systems.

Consistent with the principles that former Secretary Haig outlined in July 1981, the United States will press in the INF negotiations with all the strength, skill, and persuasion it can summon for equitable, verifiable, and global limits in theater nuclear forces at the lowest possible levels. The burden will be on the Soviet Union to move from propaganda to real arms control, to abandon its one-sided proposals, to reduce the number of these weapons in Europe, and to reach an agreement that will enhance the security of East and West alike.

The U.S. position in INF negotiations is being worked out in closest consultations with our NATO allies. In 1981, NATO's Special Consultative Group and High Level Group met regularly to establish a common Alliance view on the threat we face, NATO's needs in the nuclear area, and our arms control objectives. These Alliance consultations, of unparalleled intensity, will continue once U.S.-Soviet negotiations begin in order to insure that we pursue an agreement that is fully supported by the Alliance and that enhances the security of all its members.

A Choice of Visions

I have tried to explain how, over thirty years, a viable alternative to Moscow's view of Europe as a second-class hostage to Soviet power has been fashioned. This Atlantic alternative is built on ties of history, culture, and commerce. It shares a concept of man's place in society and of the manner in which intercourse between societies should be conducted. To survive, however, this alternative has had to create an Alliance structure that can bridge the ocean that provides its name.

The Atlantic has been spanned by the commitment to strategic unity through which each member accepts the risk of war in order to protect its allies and to secure its allies' protection. It has been spanned by the integration of conventional, theater-nuclear, and strategic forces in a single spectrum of deterrent power. It has been spanned by a strategy of flexible response, that commits the alliance to escalate a conflict as high as is needed to defeat any aggression, but permits it to confine a conflict to as low a level as possible consistent with that objective. And it has been spanned by a common commitment to seek meaningful and effective arms control.

The nuclear debate in Europe today has become a battle for the soul of Europe. The alternatives are clear. The West can reaffirm its faith in collective defense, deterrence, and serious arms control, and thus remain free. Or America can turn in upon itself, and Europe can rest its hopes for security and its prospects for freedom on Soviet goodwill. For thirty years America has rejected isolationism. For thirty years Europe has rejected Soviet patronage. For thirty years the West has instead chosen unity, strength, and freedom. There is no other choice.

Note

1. Chancellor Helmut Schmidt, "A Policy of Reliable Partnership," *Foreign Affairs* (Spring 1981), p. 747.

Appendix A: Chronology

1945
June 26 — United Nations Charter is signed in San Francisco
August 6 — Atomic bomb dropped on Hiroshima

1947
March 4 — France and the United Kingdom sign a fifty-year Treaty of Alliance and Mutual Assistance at Dunkirk
March 12 — Truman Doctrine requests direct aid to Turkey and Greece

1948
February 22 — The Czech Communist Party gains control of the government in Prague through a coup d'etat
March 17 — Brussels Treaty, a fifty-year treaty of collaboration and collective self-defense, is signed by Belgium, France, Luxembourg, Netherlands, and United Kingdom
April 16 — Organization for European Economic Cooperation (OEEC) established
June 24 — Berlin Blockade begun by USSR
September 28 — Defense Ministers of the Brussels Treaty powers decide to create a Western Union Defense Organization

1949
April 4 — North Atlantic Treaty signed by Belgium, Canada, Denmark, France, Iceland, Italy, Luxembourg, the Netherlands, Norway, Portugal, the United Kingdom, and the United States
May 5 — London Ten-Power Agreement sets up Council of Europe
May 9 — Berlin blockade lifted
August 1 — First explosion of Soviet atomic device
August 24 — North Atlantic Treaty enters into force
October 6 — Mutual Defense Assistance Act signed by Truman

1950
June 25 — North Korean forces attack the Republic of South Korea

1951

Study called Project Vista argues that the combination of relatively small ground forces with tactical nuclear weapons could hold West Europe against the Red Army.

1952
February 18   Greece and Turkey join NATO
February 20   North Atlantic Council Meeting in Lisbon reorganizes structure of the Alliance and NATO becomes a permanent organization with headquarters in Paris
May 27   Treaty signed to set up European Defense Community
October   United Kingdom explodes atomic bomb
November 1   United States explodes hydrogen bomb

1953
March 5   Stalin dies
May 28   USSR recognizes the German Democratic Republic
July 23   Korean armistice signed
August 8   USSR announces successful test of hydrogen bomb

1954
May 7   USSR bid to join NATO rejected
August 29   French National Assembly decides against ratification of the treaty to establish European Defense Community
December   North Atlantic Council authorizes military commanders to plan the use of nuclear weapons. Tactical nuclear weapons allowed to be shipped to Western Europe under U.S. custody

1955

Soviets begin deployment of Tu-16 Badger bomber
February 24   Baghdad Pact signed
May 9   Federal Republic of Germany joins NATO
May 14   USSR concludes Warsaw Pact Treaty with Albania, Bulgaria, Czechoslovakia, East Germany, Hungary, Poland, and Rumania
December   North Atlantic Council decides to equip the forces of the Alliance with atomic weapons

1956

First deployment of British Valiant bomber
First U.S. Army division intended to fight with nuclear weapons activated

	USSR begins deployment of MRBMs and nuclear-capable light and medium bombers
June 28	Riots erupt in Poland
July 26	Egypt nationalizes Suez Canal
October 23	Rebellion begins in Hungary
October 31	Franco-British intervention in Suez Canal area
November 4	Soviet suppression of Hungarian rebellion

1957

March 25	Rome Treaties signed setting up Euratom and the EEC
May 15	United Kingdom explodes hydrogen bomb
August 29	Proposals approved by all NATO countries are submitted to the London talks on disarmament
October 4	USSR launches first Sputnik
November 7	Gaither Report

1958

	First deployment of NATO F–104 nuclear capable aircraft
January 31	U.S. launches first satellite, Explorer 1
March 27	Khrushchev replaces Bulganin as head of Soviet government
May 5–7	North Atlantic Council declares it is in favor of negotiations with the Eastern bloc
December 21	Charles de Gaulle elected president of France

1959

	All five U.S. divisions stationed in Europe remodelled to fight with nuclear weapons
	First deployment of Soviet SS–4 missiles
June	de Gaulle removes 200 NATO fighter bombers with nuclear weapons from France
August 5	Foreign Ministers at Four Power Meeting in Geneva issue a statement on disarmament
August 19	Baghdad Pact becomes Central Treaty Organization

1960

	Eisenhower proposes a shared NATO nuclear force
	first deployment of British Vulcan bomber
	France explodes atomic bomb
March 15	U.N. Ten-Power Disarmament Committee starts negotiations
April	British Blue Streak IRBM program cancelled

May 16	Abortive summit meeting in Paris between United States, United Kingdom, France and USSR
June 27	Communist states withdraw from U.N. Ten-Power Disarmament negotiations
November 10	Communist leaders hold summit in Moscow and approve of Khrushchev's concept of peaceful coexistence
December 14	Organization for Economic Cooperation and Development (OECD) established

1961

	First deployment of Soviet SS-5 missiles
May 17	Kennedy announces commitment of 5 U.S. Polaris ballistic-missile submarines to NATO
June 2–3	Kennedy and Khrushchev meet in Vienna
August 13	Berlin Wall
December 13–15	Ministerial Meeting of the North Atlantic Council in Paris. The Council condemns building of the Berlin Wall and approves renewal of diplomatic contacts with the USSR

1962

	First deployment of the Pershing-1 missile, NATO F-4 fighter-bomber and British Buccaneer bomber
	First deployment of Soviet Tu-22 Blinder bomber
March 17	Seventeen nation Disarmament Conference opens in Geneva
May 4–6	Foreign Ministers and Defense Ministers of the North Atlantic Council meeting in Athens review the circumstances in which the Alliance might be compelled to have recourse to nuclear weapons (Athens Guidelines)
October	Cuban Missile Crisis
December	Skybolt missile program cancelled
December 18–20	British secure acquisition of U.S. Polaris submarines at meeting between Kennedy and Macmillan

1963

	French carrier-based aircraft deployed with nuclear capability
	First deployment of U.S. carrier-based A-6 aircraft
January	U.S. begins removal of nuclear missiles from Turkey
May 22–24	Ministerial Meeting of the North Atlantic Council in Ottawa. British Vulcan bomber and three U.S. Polaris submarines are assigned to SACEUR

July 29	de Gaulle announces that France will not sign the Moscow Treaty on a partial test ban
November 22	Kennedy assassinated
1964	
	1964 sees the demise of the Multilateral Force and the Atlantic Nuclear Force (ANF)
	USSR begins to furnish WTO members with tactical missiles minus warheads
	First deployment of French Mirage IVA and Mirage IIIE aircraft
October 15	Khruschev removed from office. Replaced by Brezhnev and Kosygin
October 16	People's Republic of China explodes atomic bomb
1965	
	First deployment of Soviet Scud SRBM
November 27	Special Committee of NATO Defense Ministers initiates study to explore ways of improving allied participation in nuclear planning
1966	
	First deployment of U.S. A-7 carrier-based aircraft
July 1	France withdraws from NATO alliance
October 27	China announces first guided-missile test
December 14	Defense Planning Committee establishes the Nuclear Defense Affairs Committee and the Nuclear Planning Group
1967	
	First deployment of U.S. F-111 E/F aircraft
June	Chinese explode hydrogen bomb
December 13-14	Defense Planning Committee adopts NATO strategic concept of flexible response
1968	
	U.S. intelligence reveals 3,500 Soviet short-range missiles and tactical weapons
May 10	Defense Planning Committee decides against development of an ABM system in Europe
June	First Polaris submarine deployed with British navy
August 20-21	Soviet and Warsaw Pact troops invade Czechoslovakia
August 25	France explodes hydrogen bomb

September 12	Albania withdraws from WTO
November 13–14	Formation of the Eurogroup

1969

The Pershing-1A replaces the Pershing-1
First deployment of Soviet SS–12 missiles

1970

April 16	SALT I talks begin
August 12	Non-Aggression Treaty between the FRG and USSR

1971

First deployment of French SSBS (IRBMs)
First deployment of French MSBS SLBMs

1972

May 26	SALT I Interim Agreement and Protocol signed
November 26	Opening of SALT II negotiations in Geneva

1973

January 1	Denmark, Ireland, and the United Kingdom join the EEC
July 3	CSCE talks begin in Helsinki
October 30	Mutual Balanced Force Reduction talks begin in Vienna

1974

First deployment of British/French Jaguar aircraft
First deployment of Backfire bomber and Su-24 Fencer attack bomber
U.S.–FRG agreement signed authorizing the use of tactical nuclear weapons in the FRG

July 16	Military *coup d'etat* in Cyprus followed by landing of Turkish troops. U.S. nuclear weapons removed from Greek and Turkish QRA aircraft
August 14	Greek forces withdraw from NATO
November 23–24	Vladivostok agreement between Ford and Brezhnev

1975

First deployment of French Pluton short-range SSM
NATO proposes nuclear weapons for tanks at MBFR

June 24	First civil-defense seminar sponsored by NATO held in Battle Creek, Michigan
August 1	Helsinki Accords on CSCE signed

1976

November 26	USSR and Warsaw Treaty states propose a no–first-use policy
December 9–10	NATO Ministers reject Soviet no–first-use proposal

1977

	French MSBS M–20 SLBMs replace older weapons
	First deployment of Soviet SS–20 missiles
May 17–18	Ministers on the Defense Planning Committee agree to set up a long-term defense program (LTDP)
June 8–9	Nuclear Planning Group meeting in Ottawa notes continuing improvements in Soviet nuclear forces, including the SS–20, and discusses current and potential improvements in NATO nuclear weapons
October 11–12	Ministers on the Nuclear Planning Group meet in Bari, Italy to establish the NPG High Level Group (HLG) on TNF modernization within the context of the LTDP
October 28	Schmidt speech to the IISS.

1978

April 7	Carter defers production of neutron bomb
April 18–19	Nuclear Planning Group endorses modernizing NATO TNF
May 23–July 1	U.N. Special Session on Disarmament

1979

April 11	Special Group established to study arms-control aspects of theater nuclear systems
June 18	SALT II signed by Carter and Brezhnev
October 6	Brezhnev offers to limit deployment of SS–20 missile if NATO would defer decision to deploy new systems
December 11–14	NATO dual decision taken to both modernize theater nuclear forces and pursue arms-control announcement that 1000 U.S. warheads would be withdrawn from Western Europe
December 21	Soviet invasion of Afghanistan

1980

	First deployment of the French Super Etendard aircraft
January 24	Special Consultative Group on Arms Control involving theater nuclear forces established
July 1	During talks in Moscow, Soviet President Brezhnev

	told Chancellor Schmidt that the Soviet Union would not persist with its insistence that NATO renounce its LRTNF-deployment plans before U.S.-Soviet negotiations could begin to seek East-West limitations on such systems
August 31	Gdansk Agreement recognizes Polish Solidarity union
September 19	The Belgian government indefinitely postpones a final decision on whether or not to accept the stationing of Cruise missiles on Belgian territory pending the development of arms-control negotiations between the United States and the USSR. The government says it will reexamine the question every six months
October 16	The United States and the USSR open preliminary talks in Geneva on theater nuclear-force limitations
October 20	Greece reintegrated into the Alliance
October 22	War breaks out between Iran and Iraq
November 4	Ronald Reagan elected President

1981

February 23	Brezhnev proposes a moratorium on deployment in Europe of new medium-range nuclear-missile systems by both NATO and the USSR
April 19	Approximately 6000 antinuclear demonstrators protest the proposed NATO LRTNF deployments at NATO headquarters outside Brussels.
June 21	The end of four-day demonstrations against NATO's TNF-modernization plans, and for a nuclear-free Europe. Demonstrations held by over 120,000 members of West Germany's major Protestant Federation
July 13	Secretary of State Haig outlines the principles of Reagan administration arms control policy: Arms control "cannot be the political centerpiece or the crucial barometer of US-Soviet relations."
August 6	Reagan authorizes full production of ERW for Lance missiles and eight-inch artillery shells to be stockpiled in the U.S.
October 2	The Italian Chamber of Deputies approves by a narrow vote, the government's plan to allow cruise-missile deployment in Sicily under the NATO TNF-modernization plan. In the United States, President Reagan announces a series of strategic-weapons decisions including the MX and B-1 bomber
October 10	Over one-quarter-million people take part in an antinuclear demonstration in Bonn

Appendix A

October 16	Reagan "limited nuclear war" remarks
October 21	Nuclear Planning Group deployment plans for NATO TNF
	U.S. Defense Secretary Weinberger agrees with the group's endorsement of a zero option as the ideal objective of negotiations with the Soviet Union
October 24	Approximately 200,000 people in Rome, and 150,000 in London gather in antinuclear protests
October 25	Antinuclear demonstrations held in Brussels, Paris, Oslo, and East Berlin
October 31	Brezhnev *Der Spiegel* interview
November 4	In testimony before the Senate Foreign Relations Committee, Secretary of State Haig says that NATO might fire a nuclear "demonstration" shot in the event of a war, to warn the Soviet Union of the risks of continuing the conflict
November 18	President Reagan announces that the United States would seek total elimination of Soviet SS–4s, SS–5s and SS–20s in return for the cancellation of NATO's deployment plans. This became the so-called zero option
November 21	Antinuclear demonstrations in Amsterdam attract over 300,000 participants
November 30	The Theater Nuclear Force Reduction Talks open in Geneva
December 6	Antinuclear demonstrations were held in a number of West European cities

1982

February	Brezhnev presents an arms control plan calling for a two-thirds reduction in nuclear weaponry in Europe
March 16	President Brezhnev announces a unilateral Soviet freeze on further developments of intermediate range forces in Europe. This includes qualitative replacement of the SS–4 and SS–5 by the SS–20. The freeze is to last until an INF agreement is reached, or until the United States begins deployment of the GLCMs and Pershing II missiles
April	At the Social Democratic Party Conference (SPD) in Germany, the Executive Committee Leadership drafts a resolution that would delay final-deployment decisions concerning the GLCM and Pershing II until the fall of 1983. The draft resolution also calls for the Geneva

	INF negotiations to eventually include British and French nuclear systems.
May 31	Spain joins NATO
June 29	Strategic Arms Reduction talks begin

Appendix B: NATO Communique, December 12, 1979

1. At a special meeting of Foreign and Defense Ministers in Brussels on December 12, 1979:

2. Ministers recalled the May 1978 Summit where governments expressed the political resolve to meet the challenges to their security posed by the continuing momentum of the Warsaw Pact military buildup.

3. The Warsaw Pact has over the years developed a large and growing capability in nuclear systems that directly threaten Western Europe and have a strategic significance for the Alliance in Europe. This situation has been especially aggravated over the last few years by Soviet decisions to implement programs modernizing and expanding their long-range nuclear capability substantially. In particular, they have deployed the SS–20 missile, which offers significant improvements over previous systems in providing greater accuracy, more mobility, and greater range, as well as having multiple warheads, and the Backfire bomber, which has a much better performance than other Soviet aircraft deployed hitherto in a theater role. During this period, while the Soviet Union has been reinforcing its superiority in Long-Range-Theater Nuclear Forces (LRTNF) both quantitatively and qualitatively, Western LRTNF capabilities have remained static. Indeed these forces are increasing in age and vulnerability and do not include land-based, long-range theater nuclear missile systems.

4. At the same time, the Soviets have also undertaken a modernization and expansion of their shorter range TNF and greatly improved the overall quality of their conventional forces. These developments took place against the background of increasing Soviet intercontinental capabilities and achievement of parity in intercontinental capability with the United States.

5. These trends have prompted serious concern within the Alliance because, if they were to continue, Soviet superiority in theater nuclear systems could undermine the stability achieved in intercontinental systems and cast doubt on the credibility of the Alliance's deterrent strategy by highlighting the gap in the spectrum of NATO's available nuclear response to aggression.

6. Ministers noted that these recent developments require concrete actions on the part of the alliance if NATO's strategy of flexible response is to remain credible. After intensive consideration, including the merits of alternative approaches, and after taking note of the positions of certain members, Ministers concluded that the overall interest of the Alliance would best be served by pursuing two parallel and complementary approaches of TNF modernization and arms control.

7. Accordingly ministers have decided to modernize NATO's LRTNF by the deployment in Europe of U.S. ground-launched systems comprising 108 Pershing II launchers, which would replace existing U.S. Pershing I-A, and 464 ground launched cruise missiles (GLCM), all with single warheads. All the nations currently participating in the integrated defense structure will participate in the program: the missiles will be stationed in selected countries and certain support costs will be met through NATO's existing common funding arrangements. The program will not increase NATO's reliance upon nuclear weapons. In this connection, Ministers agreed that as an integral part of TNF modernization, 1,000 U.S. nuclear warheads will be withdrawn from Europe as soon as feasible. Further, ministers decided that the 572 LRTNF warheads should be accommodated within that reduced level, which necessarily implies a numerical shift of emphasis away from warheads for delivery systems of other types and shorter ranges. In addition they noted with satisfaction that the Nuclear Planning Group is undertaking an examination of the precise nature, scope and basis of the adjustments resulting from the LRTNF deployment and their possible implications for the balance of roles and systems in NATO's nuclear armory as a whole. This examination will form the basis of a substantive report to NPG Ministers in the autumn of 1980.

8. Ministers attach great importance to the role of arms control in contributing to a more stable military relationship between East and West and in advancing the process of detente. This is reflected in a broad set of initiatives being examined within the Alliance to further the course of arms control and detente in the 1980s. Ministers regard arms control as an integral part of the alliance's efforts to assure the undiminished security of its member States and to make the strategic situation between East and West more stable, more predictable, and more manageable at lower levels of armaments on both sides. In this regard they welcome the contribution which the SALT II Treaty makes toward achieving these objectives.

9. Ministers consider that, building on this accomplishment and taking account of the expansion of Soviet LRTNF capabilities of concern to NATO, arms control efforts to achieve a more stable overall nuclear balance at lower levels of nuclear weapons on both sides should therefore now include certain United States and Soviet long-range theater nuclear systems.

This would reflect previous Western suggestions to include such Soviet and U.S. systems in arms control negotiations and more recent expressions by Soviet President Brezhnev of willingness to do so. Ministers fully support the decision taken by the United States following consultations within the Alliance to negotiate arms limitations on LRTNF and to propose to the USSR to begin negotiations as soon as possible along the following lines which have been elaborated in intensive consultations within the alliance:

a. Any future limitations on U.S. systems principally designed for theater

Appendix B 133

missions should be accompanied by appropriate limitations on Soviet theater systems.

b. Limitations on United States and Soviet long-range theater nuclear systems should be negotiated bilaterally in the SALT II framework in a step-by-step approach.
c. The immediate objective of these negotiations should be the establishment of agreed limitations on United States and Soviet land-based long-range theater nuclear missile systems.
d. Any agreed limitations on these systems must be consistent with the principle of equality between the sides. Therefore, the limitations should take the form of de jure equality both in ceilings and in rights.
e. Any agreed limitations must be adequately verifiable.

10. Given the special importance of these negotiations for the overall security of the Alliance, a special consultative body at a high level will be constituted within the Alliance to support the U.S. negotiating effort. This body will follow the negotiations on a continuous basis and report to the Foreign and Defense Ministers who will examine developments in these negotiations as well as in other arms control negotiations at their semiannual meetings.

11. The Ministers have decided to pursue these two parallel and complementary approaches in order to avert an arms race in Europe caused by the Soviet TNF buildup, yet preserve the viability of NATO's strategy of deterrence and defense and thus maintain the security of its member States.

a. A modernization decision, including a commitment to deployments, is necessary to meet NATO's deterrence and defense needs, to provide a credible response to unilateral Soviet TNF deployments, and to provide the foundation for the pursuit of serious negotiations on TNF.
b. Success of arms control in constraining the Soviet buildup can enhance Alliance security, modify the scale of NATO's TNF requirements, and promote stability and detente in Europe in consonance with NATO's basic policy of deterrence, defense and detente as enunciated in the Harmel Report. NATO's TNF requirements will be examined in the light of concrete results reached through negotiations.

Appendix C: NATO Communique, December 14, 1979

The North Atlantic Council met in Ministerial session in Brussels on December 13 and 14, 1979.

Ministers accepted with pleasure the invitation of the Turkish Government to hold the next Ministerial session of the North Atlantic Council in Ankara in the spring of 1980.

Ministers renewed their faith in the North Atlantic Treaty which guarantees the freedom, security and well-being of the peoples and the preservation of peace and international stability. Because their governments are based on the consent of their peoples, on democratic institutions and on the principle of equality and the rule of law, the members of the Alliance have the strength, enchanced by the will to assist each other, to face the challenges which lie ahead. Looking forward to the 1980s, Ministers expressed their confidence that, by maintaining the strength and cohesion of their Alliance and pursuing the complementary goals of arms control, disarmament, and the improvement of relations between East and West in general, their governments would continue to make a major contribution to peace and stability in Europe and the world.

Reviewing developments in East-West relations since they last met, Ministers noted that the conclusion of the study undertaken in 1978 remain valid. They recalled their commitment to détente and stressed the defensive nature of the Alliance. Events since their previous meeting showed the continuing influence of forces not conducive to the consolidation of international stability and security. They expressed concern over the direct or indirect actions of the Soviet Union and some of its Allies in a number of troubled areas concurrently with a very considerable build-up, both qualitative and quantitative, in Warsaw Pact military strength, and particularly with growing Soviet theatre nuclear and conventional capabilities. Ministers noted that these developments were a cause for legitimate disquiet and were not compatible either with assurances by the Warsaw Pact countries that they do not seek military superiority or with their publicly-declared intention to promote detente, particularly in the military sphere. Ministers reiterated their view that detente must be worldwide and indivisible in character.

Ministers confirmed that their governments were resolved to take steps to reduce the growing imbalance of forces by improving their military capabilities and thus maintain an adequate level of deterrence and defense across the full spectrum. They recalled the determination of their governments to achieve, as a key element in conventional force modernization, more effective use of available resources through cooperative equipment programs and increased standardization and interoperability of weapons systems. They noted with satisfaction the initial progress that has been achieved in these respects, they repeated that through the transatlantic dialog they would continue to work toward more balanced relations among the European and North American members of the alliance in the field of armaments development and production in order to enhance the availability and quality of new defense equipment. They noted the contribution which is being made by the Conference of National Armaments Directors in this respect, and the need to bear in mind the interests of the less industrialized members of the alliance.

Ministers believed that efforts to achieve agreement in fields of arms control, disarmament and confidence building should go hand in hand with defense efforts of the allies. They noted that recent proposals put forward by the Eastern countries echoed in part of the Western proposals and they saw in them a hopeful indication of the evolution of these countries toward a more positive attitude in the search for common ground. Ministers considered ways of advancing appropriate discussions and negotiations.

Ministers recalled that the Strategic Arms Limitation Treaty (SALT II) signed by the United States and the Soviet Union on June 18 reflected their desire for genuine arms control measures which should contribute to the stability of East-West relations. Ministers observed that the treaty makes it possible to maintain a strong U.S. strategic nuclear deterrent, which remains vital to the defense of the alliance. Thus this treaty, which will have the effect of curbing the buildup of strategic nuclear weapons in the world, improves the prospects for detente without jeopardizing the security interests of the members of the alliance. Ministers expressed the hope that the treaty would soon come into force. They looked forward to the early continuation of the SALT process, on the basis of further close consultations within the alliance, leading to additional United States and Soviet reductions and qualitative limitations in the nuclear field. They also expressed the belief that ratification of the treaty would contribute to other possibilities of progress in the field of arms control.

Ministers believed that the process initiated by the Conference on Security and Cooperation in Europe made a most valuable contribution to the strengthening of detente, and offered further opportunities to develop existing and new areas of dialog in the search for agreement. They expressed the hope that the CSCE followup meeting to be held at Madrid in 1980 will be a major step forward in that process. Tangible progress in the meantime in implementing the principles and provisions of the Final Act and adequate preparation are of great importance for the success of the Madrid meeting and could provide a basis for participation at the political level. Although there have been certain welcome measures of relief, in particular the granting of amnesty, and some improvement in other fields, Ministers noted with concern that in certain countries the situation remained unsatisfactory or had even deteriorated as regards respect for human rights and fundamental freedoms, including cases where citizens continue to be subject to harassment and imprisonment for no reason other than their efforts to bring about the full implementation of the Final Act. Ministers also noted that progress in the field of human contacts was uneven and expressed their concern that the level of implementation of the provisions dealing with a freer flow of information and working conditions for journalists had remained low and, in some cases, had deteriorated. They noted with satisfaction, however, that the Final Act increasingly has become the standard by which the actions of signatory states are judged.

Ministers expressed their intention to devote increasing efforts to preparations for the Madrid meeting during the period ahead, emphasizing the importance of consultations among allies as well as with the other participating states and of maintaining balance among all sections of the Final Act. They confirmed that they intended to approach and conduct the Madrid meeting in a constructive frame of mind and in a manner which would permit a thorough, frank and measured review of the implementation of all provisions of the Final Act. In this spirit, they will be ready to put forward new proposals and to discuss proposals from other participants calculated to bring concrete and balanced progress in all fields covered by the Final Act and thereby contribute to the vitality of the CSCE process. Ministers recognized the importance for the alliance of developing the confidence-building measures and the other provisions of the Final Act relating to certain aspects of security and disarmament, and hoped for concrete results in this regard at the Madrid meeting.

They reviewed with interest the proposals made in these fields by different CSCE participants, whether Western, neutral and nonaligned, or Warsaw Pact countries, including those made by the latter in May and December 1979. They considered that the proposal for a Conference on Disarmament in Europe put forward by France is a useful concept providing a basis upon which to continue developing their approach in this field to bring about such a conference.

They agreed to work toward the adoption during the Madrid meeting, as part of a balanced outcome, of a mandate for further negotiations under the aegis of the CSCE on military significant and verifiable confidence-building measures, applicable to the entire continent of Europe. These, if agreed, would help create conditions conducive to limitation and reduction of arms in the same geographical area. This process should take account of both the varied aspects of the existing security situation and of the current negotiations on other aspects of arms control and disarmament concerning the European continent.

The Ministers of countries participating in the negotiations and mutual and balanced force reductions reemphasized their determination to work for a successful outcome which would enhance stability, peace, and security in Europe. They noted, however, their concern that despite representations made at the highest level by Western leaders to the Eastern participants, the East has made no effort to revolve the data question. These Ministers noted that agreement on the starting size of forces to be reduced is not only an essential prerequisite to any reductions, but can also serve to build confidence that a reduction agreement is being observed and that mutual security is being enhanced.

In order to advance the negotiations toward an early result, these Ministers approved a proposal for an interim phase I agreement consistent with the objectives of their governments in thenegotiations, in particular the establishment of parity in the form of an agreement on a combined common collective ceiling on air and ground force manpower of each side in the area of reductions. Their new initiative aims at simplifying existing proposals for a phase I agreement by focusing on United States and Soviet manpower withdrawals and limitations, based on agreed United States-Soviet data, and on associated measures applied on a multilateral basis. This interim phase I agreement would open the way for a subsequent phase II agreement, based on agreed overall data, providing for a common collective ceiling on ground force manpower for each side at approximately 700,000 and for agreement on a combined common collective ceiling on air and ground force manpower for each side at approximately 900,000.

These Ministers called attention to the package of associated measures which forms an integral part of their proposal for an interim phase I agreement. This package of measures is designed to promote military stability and confidence, to insure adequate verification of an MBFR agreement, and to help safeguard undiminished security for flank countries.

These Ministers urged Eastern participants to give prompt and serious consideration to their initiative, which takes account of negotiating proposals of both sides and which is in accordance with the agreed aim of the negotiations to contribute to the creation of a more stable relationship and to the strengthening of peace and security in Europe. They view this new Western initiative as an integral part of the arms control initiatives agreed upon during this ministerial meeting.

Turning to the question of negotiations on disarmament and arms limitations in other forums, Ministers reaffirmed the importance which they attached to the adoption of effective, balanced, and verifiable measures. They welcomed as positive elements the discussions during the first session of the Committee on Disarmament in Geneva and the deliberations of the Disarmament Commission in New York. They attached importance to the frequent and active consultation on these questions within the permanent machinery of the Alliance.

Appendix C

Ministers discussed developments with regard to Berlin and Germany as a whole. They noted that since their last meeting the climate in and around Berlin had continued to remain relatively calm. Ministers reaffirmed their conviction that an undisturbed situation in Berlin and on the access routes is an essential element of detente, security, and cooperation in Europe, and noted the continuing relevance of the London declaration of May 9, 1977, and the Tokyo declaration of June 29, 1979. Ministers noted with satisfaction the improved climate in relations between the two German states after a period of reserve and welcomed the conclusion of new agreements and the continuation of negotiations. Ministers consider this as a positive element in the process of detente in Europe, having at the same time beneficial effects for Berlin.

Ministers noted the report on the situation in the Mediterranean prepared on their instructions and underlined again the necessity of maintaining the balance of forces in the whole area. They requested the council in permanent session to continue to consult on the question and submit a further report at their next meeting.

Ministers welcomed the continuation of dialogue between Greece and Turkey in search of a peaceful solution to the differences between the two countries and they expressed the hope that in this manner positive results could be attained in the near future.

Ministers considered a report by the Secretary General on the particular problems faced by the economically less advanced member countries which constitutes a sound basis for action. While noting with satisfaction the special efforts that had been made over recent months, they stressed the need to give further momentum to the efforts to provide, in the spirit of article 2 of the North Atlantic Treaty, assistance to those countries, so as to reach concrete and timely results. They reaffirmed their continuing political support for this process which will, indeed, constitute an essential element for the fulfillment of the contribution by those countries to collective defense.

With respect to the Middle East, the Ministers affirmed the importance of elaborating and implementing a just, lasting, and comprehensive settlement of the Arab-Israel conflict on the basis of Resolutions 242 and 338 and with the participation of all the parties concerned, including representatives of the Palestinian people. Ministers noted with satisfaction the progress achieved by Egypt and Israel in the implementation of Resolution 242 insofar as their mutual relations are concerned. They reaffirmed that a lasting peace requires the solution of the Palestinian problem in all its aspects and the achievement of the legitimate rights of the Palestinian people in the context of a negotiated settlement that insures the security of all states in the region including Israel.

Ministers warmly welcomed the agreement reached in the constitutional conference on Rhodesia. They expressed the hope that the cease-fire proposals agreed at the conference would quickly become fully effective, and that peace would return to Rhodesia and the neighboring countries. Ministers looked forward to the day when the independent Republic of Zimbabwe would take its place as a full member of the international community.

Ministers, recalling that the Committee on the Challenges of Modern Society (CCMS) having been set up in 1969, took note of the Committee's achievements during its first 10 years. They commended its innovative and flexible approach to the many problems of the human environment in fields such as energy conservation, alternative energy sources and pollution. Ministers noted the studies launched in 1979, including those of the restoration and conservation of monuments, and on man's impact on the stratosphere, as well as projected studies on the management of technology.

The Ministers who participated in the special meeting of Foreign and Defense Ministers on December 12, 1979, noted with satisfaction that the decisions taken today by the North Atlantic Council in their opinion complemented those adopted at that meeting. Taken together, along with continuing activities flowing from decisions reached at the London and Washington meetings, they constitute a comprehensive program of action. This program comprises measures to reduce the military imbalance through concrete improvement and modernization of long-range theater nuclear and conventional forces, and the following wide range of initiatives particularly in the fields of confidence building and arms control designed to improve mutual security and cooperation in Europe:

An offer to negotiate for substantial reductions in the level of long-range theater nuclear forces as well as intercontinental strategic forces within the framework of SALT III:

> Unilateral withdrawal of 1,000 U.S. nuclear warheads from Europe as part of the December 12 decision;
>
> A proposal for an interim phase I agreement for Mutual and Balanced Force Reductions, designed to give fresh impetus to the MBFR negotiations;
>
> A proposal for a package of associated measures in MBFR designed to insure compliance with the agreement and to make military activities more transparent, thereby improving mutual confidence;
>
> In furtherance of the CSCE process, readiness to examine proposals concerning Confidence-Building Measures and a Conference on Disarmament in Europe.

These Ministers are determined that the 1980s should see a fundamental change for the better in the situation between East and West and will make every effort to bring this about. The program of action which they envisage offers the best opportunity for creating more constructive relations between East and West for which their citizens have hoped for so long.

These Ministers considered that this program represents a major new opportunity for the countries of the Warsaw Pact to translate into action the interest they have signaled in improving the situation in Europe. They call on the Warsaw Pact governments to respond to this offer by making a determined effort in all available negotiating forums, to achieve substantial results which will enhance security and mutual trust.

Glossary

Air superiority Denial of enemy use of the air to attack friendly air or ground targets.

Artillery fired atomic projectiles (AFAP) Artillery shells that produce nuclear explosions.

Atomic demolition munitions (ADM) Mines that product nuclear explosions. Used to create land barriers in the path of enemy forces.

A–6 Navy/Marine Corps night/bad weather attack aircraft based on aircraft carriers. Nuclear-capable A–6s comprise part of American Forward-Based Systems (FBS—see Forward-Based Systems).

A–7 Navy/Air Force attack aircraft based on aircraft carriers. Nuclear-capable A–7s comprise part of American Forward-Based Systems.

A–10 Air Force attack aircraft designed mainly for close air support.

Battlefield nuclear weapon Very short-range nuclear weapons, including missiles and artillery projectiles, used to influence the outcome of a particular battle.

Close air support Air attacks on enemy ground forces in contact with friendly ground forces.

Collateral damage Unintended damage to civilian facilities or casualties to civilian personnel incurred as a consequence of a nuclear strike against a different, usually military, target.

Coupling The linkage between American strategic forces and NATO nuclear forces. Some Europeans fear decoupling, that is, that the United States might fight a nuclear war in Europe without using its United States-based forces and without putting U.S. cities at risk.

Cruise missile A pilotless missile, propelled by an air-breathing jet engine, that flies in the atmosphere. Although cruise missiles fly only at subsonic speeds, their advanced guidance system allows them to fly very low and makes them extremely accurate. Cruise missiles may be armed with either conventional or nuclear warheads and launched from an aircraft, submarine, surface ship, or land-based platform.

Dual-capable system A weapon system capable of carrying nuclear or conventional explosives.

Dual-key system A command and control system that insures that a host country's nuclear weapons will not be launched without American consent.

Dual-mission system A weapon system that can operate in a tactical, theater, or strategic mode. Sometimes called a "gray-area" or "hybrid" system.

Enhanced radiation warhead (ERW)   A warhead, commonly referred to as the neutron bomb, that kills more by radiation than by blast. This warhead is designed for deployment on the European-based U.S. Lance missile, and on certain field-artillery projectiles.

Escalation dominance   The ability of one side in a conflict to gain a net military advantage by going to the next higher level of force. For example, the United States would have escalation dominance over the Soviets if it could improve its military position by going from using battlefield nuclear weapons to using intermediate-range nuclear weapons.

Extended deterrence   The extension of the American nuclear umbrella to areas such as Western Europe, Japan, and South Korea. Any Soviet aggression in these areas would carry the risk of escalation to U.S. use of nuclear weapons, ultimately involving attacks on the Soviet homeland.

Forward-based system (FBS)   Medium-range U.S. nuclear-delivery systems, based in third countries or on aircraft carriers, that can strike targets in the Soviet Union. Examples of such systems are F–111 and F–4 ground-based aircraft and carrier-based A–6 and A–7.

F–4   Air Force/Navy/Marine Corps fighter/attack aircraft based both on land and on aircraft carriers.

F–111   Air Force night/bad weather attack aircraft based on land. European-based, nuclear-capable versions comprise part of American Forward-Based Systems (FBS).

Graduated response   An effort to slow or prevent escalation of an armed conflict by responding to adversary actions at a similar or only slightly higher level of force.

Ground-launched cruise missile (GLCM)   A cruise missile launched from ground installations or vehicles.

High level group (HLG)   A group formed by the NATO leadership in 1977 composed of senior defense ministry officials who meet regularly. The group has studied deficiencies in the Alliance theater nuclear posture given the onset of strategic parity, the modernization of Soviet Theater Nuclear Forces, and the growing obsolescence of existing NATO Theater Nuclear Forces.

Honest John   A short-range unguided truck-mounted rocket, intended to deliver a nuclear weapon against enemy combat forces. Currently being phased out of the U.S. arsenal.

Interdiction   Air-to-ground attacks on enemy forces, logistics, or facilities behind the battle lines.

Intermediate-nuclear forces (INF)   A relatively new term coined originally by U.S. officials to emphasize the links between U.S. strategic weapons and theater weapons in Europe. In its original meaning it was synonymous with Long-Range-Theater Nuclear Forces (LRTNF). More recently it has been expanded to include all TNF except battlefield weapons. (*See also* Theater Nuclear Forces, Long-Range-Theater Nuclear Forces.)

Glossary

Intermediate-range ballistic missile (IRBM) A ballistic missile with a range of 1500 to 4000 nautical miles.

Lance A newer short-range inertially guided tactical missile mounted on a tracked vehicle or trailer, capable of delivering a nuclear weapon against enemy combat forces.

Long-range-theater nuclear forces (LRTNF) Missiles and bombers deployed in a particular theater that have ranges between approximately 600 miles and 4,000 miles. (*See also* Intermediate-nuclear forces.)

Massive retaliation The strategy of the Eisenhower administration, which sought to deter aggression by the threat of all-out nuclear war, instead of by reliance on conventional defense.

Medium-range ballistic missile (MRBM) A ballistic missile with a range of 500 to 1500 nautical miles.

Multi-lateral force (MLF) A plan developed in the early 1960s, but never implemented, that would have placed ballistic missiles on surface ships with crews made up of members of the NATO Alliance. The plan was designed to allow European members of the Alliance to have some control of nuclear weapons.

Mutually balanced force-reduction talks (MBFR) Currently ongoing negotiations between NATO and Warsaw Pact representatives concerning military force reductions in Europe.

No-first-use doctrine A no first use pledge by a nation obliges it not to introduce nuclear weapons first into a conflict. (*See* First use.)

Nuclear-capable artillery Cannon artillery capable of firing atomic projectiles. (*See* Artillery-fired atomic projectiles.)

Nuclear operations plan (NOP) The plan developed by the Supreme Allied Commander, Europe, for the execution of nuclear strikes with the nuclear weapons under his command.

Nuclear planning group (NPG) One of two permanent bodies within the NATO Alliance established in 1966, and charged with NATO nuclear planning. As of 1979, all thirteen members of the alliance participate in the Group on a regular basis.

Permissive-action link (PAL) A coded device attached to nuclear weapons deployed abroad that impedes the unauthorized arming or firing of the weapon.

Pershing IA A truck-mounted, inertially guided short-range missile capable of delivering a nuclear weapon against enemy-area targets. Pershing IA is mobile, solid-fueled, and capable of hitting points within 1200 feet of its target. Currently, 108 are deployed with the United States Army in Germany, along with seventy-two attached to the FRG Air Force. Pershing IA is to be replaced by the Pershing II missile, starting in 1983.

Pershing II (PII) Scheduled to begin deployment in 1983, the Pershing II is the successor system to the Pershing IA SRBM. The Pershing II incorporates the new RADAG guidance system, making it an extremely accurate and mobile weapon. 108 Pershing II missiles are to be deployed in Germany. *See* Radar area-correlator guidance—RADAG.)

Poseidon C3   The second generation of submarine-launched ballistic missiles (SLBM). Each Poseidon missile has a range of 2500 nautical miles and is armed with ten warheads with a yield of fifty kilotons.

Quick-reaction alert (QRA)   A condition in which specified numbers of aircraft and missiles are readied to deliver designated nuclear strikes on very short notice.

Radar Area-Correlator Guidance (RADAG)   A guidance principle that compares a radar image of terrain along the reentry-vehicle flight path with an image of the target area stored in an onboard computer and that makes corrections in the reentry-vehicle flight to establish correspondence between the two images and accurately strike the target. This system helps give Pershing IIs their high accuracy.

Sea-launched cruise missiles (SLCM)   A cruise missile launched either from submarines or surface ships.

Sergeant   A truck-mounted, short-range tactical missile capable of delivering a nuclear weapon against enemy combat forces. It is being phased out of U.S. inventory.

Short-range ballistic missile (SRBM)   A ballistic missile with a range of less than 500 nautical miles.

Special ammunition-storage sites (SAS)   Storage facilities for nuclear weapons deployed abroad.

Special group (SG)   A group established in 1979 and composed of high-level foreign-ministry personnel, whose aim was to study the arms control implications of Theater Nuclear Forces. This group has been replaced by the Special Consultative Group, which coordinates arms control approaches to the INF issue.

Strategic   The term used to denote those weapons or forces capable of directly affecting another nation's war-fighting ability, as distinguished from tactical, or theater weapons, or forces.

Strategic arms-limitation talks (SALT)   Talks between the United States and the USSR that were initiated in 1969 and seek to limit the strategic forces, both offensive and defensive, of both sides.

Strategic arms-reduction talks (START)   The name given by President Reagan to the talks on limiting strategic weapons in 1981. The change in name from SALT came as a result of the administration's desire to emphasize reductions of strategic weapons on both sides.

Supreme allied commander—Europe (SACEUR)   The U.S. Army designation for the chief military commander of allied forces in Europe (United States and NATO forces).

SS–4/SS–5   SS–4 and SS–5 comprised the early generation Soviet INF.

Both of these IRBMs are liquid fueled, and carry warheads in the range of one megaton. They are now being replaced by the SS–20 missile.

SS–20 The new generation Soviet intermediate nuclear missile system. Solid fueled and mobile, the SS–20 carries three MIRVed warheads, each in the range of 150 kilotons. Its accuracy is 0.26 nautical miles.

Tactical Relating to battlefield operations as distinguished from theater or strategic operations. Tactical weapons or forces are those designed for combat with opposing military forces, rather than for reaching the rear or home areas of the opponent.

Tactical nuclear weapon (TNW) A short-range, low-yield nuclear weapon designed for combat use on the battlefield.

Theater (of operations) A distinct area of operations including, but not limited to, tactical operations and encompassing all land, sea, and air activities within that zone. Designating a given area as a theater of war is an administrative, logistical, and command convenience and may vary from one nation to another or may be agreed upon among allies. A theater includes the rear areas of the combat forces, but not necessarily their homelands. Their responsibilities may be assigned in the absence of war.

Theater nuclear forces (TNF) Those nuclear forces deployed and intended for use in a particular geographic region, such as Europe or the Pacific. (*See also* Intermediate nuclear forces.)

Bibliography

Arms Control in Europe

Abley, Mark. "From Poland to Portugal, the Disarming of Europe." *Canadian Forum,* August 1981: 7–13.
Birnbaum, Karl E., ed. *Arms Control in Europe: Problems and Prospects.* Laxenburg, Austria: Austrian Institute for International Affairs, no. 1, March 1980.
Borowski, John. "Arms Control in Europe: Building Confidence." *The Bulletin of the Atomic Scientists,* January 1982: 45–47.
_____. "East-West Bargaining on Theater Nuclear Forces." *Parameters,* September 1981: 31–38.
_____. "Towards Theater Nuclear Arms Control?" *The Washington Quarterly.* Winter 1980: 100–125.
Brent, Mark, and William H. Kincade. "NATO Decides: New Arms and Arms Control in Europe." *Arms Control Today.* February 1980: 1–2, 6–10.
Buchan, Alastair, and Windsor, Philip. *Arms and Stability in Europe.* New York: Praeger Publishers, 1963.
Bundy, McGeorge, "Instead of Missiles." *The New York Times.* May 21, 1981.
Buteux, Paul. "Theater Nuclear Forces: Modernization Plan and Arms Control Initiative." *NATO Review.* December 1980: 1–6.
Carnegie Panel on U.S. Security and the Future of Arms Control. *Challenges for U.S. National Security: Assessing the Balance: Defense Spending and Conventional Forces, Part 2.* Washington, D.C.: Carnegie Endowment for International Peace, 1981.
Carnegie Panel on U.S. Security and the Future of Arms Control, *Challenges for U.S. National Security: Nuclear Strategy Issues of the 1980s: Strategic Vulnerabilities, Command, Control, Communications, and Intelligence, and Theater Nuclear Forces, Part 3,* Washington, D.C.: Carnegie Endowment for International Peace, 1982.
Corterier, Peter. "Modernization of Theater Nuclear Forces and Arms Control." *NATO Review.* August 1981: 4–9.
Crollen, Luc. "NATO and Arms Control." *NATO Review.* October 1980: 20–23.
Czempiel, Ernst-Otto; Krell, Gert; Muller, Herald; and Rode, Reinhard, eds. *United States Interests and Western Europe: Arms Control, Energy and Trade.* Frankfurt: Campus Verlag GmbH, 1981.

Davis, Lynn E. "A Proposal for TNF Arms Control." *Survival.* November/December 1981: 242–245.
de Vries, Klaas G. "Responding to the SS–20: An Alternative Approach." *Survival.* November/December 1979: 251–255.
Eagleburger, Lawrence. "The U.S. Approach to the Negotiations on Intermediate Range Nuclear Forces." *NATO Review.* Feburary 1982: 7–11.
Freedman, Lawrence. "The Dilemma of Theater Nuclear Arms Control." *Survival.* January/February 1981: 2–10.
Frye, Alton. "Nuclear Weapons in Europe: No Exit From Ambivalence." *Survival.* May/June 1981: 98–106.
Garthoff, Raymond. "Brezhnev's Opening: The TNF Tangle." *Foreign Policy.* Winter 1980–1981: 82–94.
Goetze, Bernd A. "Security Through Arms Control: A New Realism for the 1980s." *NATO Review.* April 1980: 17–21.
Haig, Alexander. *Arms Control for the 1980s: An American Policy.* Washington, D.C.: U.S. Department of State, Bureau of Public Affairs, July 14, 1981. (Address by Secretary of State Haig before the Foreign Policy Association in New York on July 14, 1981.)
Hanmer, Stephen R., Jr. "NATO's Long Range Theater Nuclear Forces: Modernization in Parallel with Arms Control." *NATO Review.* February 1980: 1–6.
Higgins, Michael, and Makins, Christopher. "Theater Nuclear Forces and 'Gray Area' Arms Control." *Continuity and Change in the Eighties and Beyond: Proceedings of the National Security Affairs Conference.* Washington, D.C.: National Defense University Press, November 1979, 29–48.
Krell, Gert. "The Debate About LRTNF Modernization: A Case for Arms Control." *Friedensforschung Aktuell.* Frankfurt: The Peace Research Institute of Frankfurt, Germany, November 1, 1981.
Lellouche, Pierre. *Long Range Theater Nuclear Forces in Europe: Prospects for Meaningful Negotiations.* Paris: Institute Francais des Relations Internationales, March 1981.
Linebaugh, David. "The Case for Moratorium." *St. Louis Post Dispatch.* June 2, 1981.
McGraw Olive, Marsha, and Porro, Jeffrey D. *Nuclear Weapons in Europe: Modernization and Limitation.* Lexington, Mass.: Lexington Books, D.C. Heath and Co., 1982.
Makins, Christopher. "Negotiating European Security: The Next Steps." *Survival.* November/December 1979: 256–263.
Metzger, Robert, and Doty, Paul. "Arms Control Enters the Gray Area." *International Security.* Winter, 1978/9: 17–52.
Nitze, Paul. "The Relationship of Strategic and Theater Nuclear Forces." *International Security.* Fall 1977: 122–131.

Nunn, Sam. "Arms Control and Theater Nuclear Force Modernization." *The Atlantic Community Quarterly.* Winter 1979/80: 437–444.

Owen, David. "Negotiate and Survive." *Face the Future.* London: The Fabian Society, 1980.

Ranger, Robert. "An Alternative Future for MBFR: A European Arms Control Conference." *Survival.* July/August 1979: 164–171.

Ranger, Robin. "NATO's New Great Debate: Theater Nuclear Force Modernization and Arms Control." *International Journal,* Summer 1981: 556–574.

Reagan, Ronald. *U.S. Program for Peace and Arms Control.* Washington: U.S. Department of State, Bureau of Public Affairs, November 18, 1981.

Richardson, Elliot, and Simonet, Henri. "Nuclear Weapons in Europe." *Arms Control Today.* November 1981: 1–3, 8–10.

Rostow, Eugene V. *Prospects for Arms Control.* Washington, D.C.: U.S. Department of State, Bureau of Public Affairs, October 21, 1981.

Sharp, Jane M.O. "Four Approaches to an INF Agreement." *Arms Control Today.* March 1982: 1–3, 6–8.

Sloan, Stanley R. *NATO's Theater Nuclear Forces: Modernization and Arms Control.* Congressional Research Service, Issue Brief 81128m, July 29, 1981.

Treverton, Gregory F."Nuclear Weapons and the Gray Area." *Foreign Affairs.* February 1980: 1075–1089.

U.S. Executive Offices. *Fiscal Year 1983 Arms Control Impact Statements.* Washington, D.C.: U.S. Government Printing Office. 1982.

European Security

Barnaby, Frank. "Europe Aroused." *The Bulletin of Atomic Scientists.* February 1982: 8–9.

Bertram, Christoph. "The Implications of Theater Nuclear Weapons in Europe." *Foreign Affairs.* Winter 1981/82: 305–326.

Brans, Wilhelm. *The NATO Two-Track Decision and German/German Relations.* Bonn: Study Group on Security and Disarmament in the Friedrich-Ebert-Stiftung Research Institute, 1981.

Brzezinski, Zbigniew. "Defense and Detente." *The Atlantic Community Quarterly.* Winter 1979/80: 385–389.

DePorte, A.W. *Europe Between the Super-Powers: The Enduring Balance.* New Haven, Conn: Yale University Press, 1979.

de Rose, Francois. "The Future of SALT and Western Security in Europe." *Foreign Affairs.* February 1980: 1065–1074.

de Vries, Klaas G. *General Report on Atlantic Security Issues.* Brussels: North Atlantic Assembly, November 1980.

Eagleburger, Lawrence S. *Preserving Western Independence and Security.* Washington, D.C.: U.S. Department of State, Bureau of Public Affairs, October 15, 1981.

Forrestall, Michael. *General Report on Alliance Security in the 1980s.* Brussels: North Atlantic Assembly International Secretariat, October 1981.

Freedman, Lawrence, "NATO Myths." *Foreign Policy.* Winter 1981/82: 48–68.

Hoffman, Stanley. "NATO and Nuclear Weapons: Reasons and Unreason," *Foreign Affairs.* Winter 1981/82: 327–346.

Institute for Foreign Policy Analysis. *Report of the Fourth German-American Roundtable on NATO: NATO Modernization and European Security.* Bonn: Federal Republic of Germany, December 12–13, 1980.

Kennan, George F. "Europe's Problems, Europe's Choices." *Foreign Policy.* Spring 1974: 3–16.

Kissinger, Henry. "The Future of NATO." *The Washington Quarterly.* January 16, 1980.

Knorr, Klaus, ed. *NATO and American Security.* Princeton, N.J.: Princeton University Press, 1959.

Leebaert, Derek. *European Security: Prospects for the 1980s.* Lexington, Mass.: Lexington Books, D.C. Heath and Co., 1979.

Lellouche, Pierre. "Europe and Her Defense." *Foreign Affairs.* Spring 1981: 813–834.

Morgan, Michael. "NATO's Nuclear Debate." *Defense and Foreign Digest.* November 2, 1980.

Myers, Kenneth A. ed. *NATO-The Next Thirty Years: The Changing Political, Economic and Military Setting.* Boulder, Colo.: Westview Press, 1980.

NATO Final Communiques 1975–1980. Brussels: NATO Information Service, 1981.

"NATO, Nuclear Weapons, and the Death of Detente." *The Defense Monitor.* March 1980: 1–8.

Nunn, Sam. "Deterring War in Europe." *NATO Review.* February 1977: 4–7.

Osgood, Robert E. *NATO: The Entangling Alliance.* Chicago: University of Chicago Press, 1962.

Pierre, Andrew J. *Nuclear Politics: The British Experience with an Independent Strategic Force 1939-1970.* London: Oxford University Press, 1972.

Rush, Kenneth; Scowcroft, Brent; and Wolf, Joseph J. "The Credibility of the NATO Deterrent." *NATO Review.* October 1981: 7–13.

U.S. Congress. House. Committee on Foreign Affairs. *Western Security Issues: European Perspectives.* Washington, D.C.: U.S. Government Printing Office, 1979.

U.S. Congress. Senate. Committee on Foreign Relations. Subcommittee on European Affairs. *SALT and the NATO Allies.* Washington, D.C.: U.S. Government Printing Office, 1979.
U.S. Congress. Senate. Committee on Foreign Relations. Subcommittee on U.S. Security Agreements and Commitments Abroad. *U.S. Security Issues in Europe: Burden Sharing and Offset, MBFR and Nuclear Weapons.* Washington, D.C.: U.S. Government Printing Office, September 1973.
Vance, Cyrus. *Strengthening NATO's Defense.* Washington, D.C.: Department of State, Bureau of Public Affairs, December 12, 1979.
Warnke, Paul C. "Theater Nuclear Forces and NATO Security." *Orbis.* Fall 1981: 501–504.

NATO Modernization and Nuclear Strategy

Betts, Richard K. "Hedging Against Surprise Attack." *Survival.* July/August 1981: 146–156.
———. "Surprise Attack: NATO's Political Vulnerability." *International Security.* Spring 1981: 117–149.
Brandt, Richard. "When is it Morally Permissable to Use Tactical Nuclear Weapons?" *Parameters.* September 1981: 75–80.
Brenner, Michael J. "Tactical Nuclear Strategy and European Defence: A Critical Appraisal." *International Affairs.* January 1975.
Cartwright, John, and Critchley, Julian. *Interim Report of the Special Committee on Nuclear Weapons in Europe.* Brussels: North Atlantic Assembly, International Secretariat, October 1981.
Collins, Arthur S. Jr. "Tactical Nuclear Warfare and NATO: Viable Strategy or Dead End?" *NATO's Fifteen Nations.* June/July 1976: 72–87.
Credibility of the NATO Deterrent: Bringing the NATO Deterrent Up to Date. The Atlantic Council's Working Group on the Credibility of the NATO Deterrent, May 1981.
Davis, Jacquelyn K. "Theater Nuclear Force Modernization and NATO's Flexible Response Strategy." *The Annals of the American Academy of Political and Social Science.* September 1981: 78–87.
de Rose, Francois. "Updating Deterrence in Europe: Inflexible Response?" *Survival.* January/February 1982: 19–23.
Gliksman, Alex. "Three Keys for Europe's Bombs." *Foreign Policy.* Summer 1980: 40–57.
Ikle, Fred Charles. "NATO's 'First Nuclear Use': A Deepening Trap?" *Strategic Review.* Winter 190: 18–23.
Jarvenpaa, Pauli. "The Concept of Limited Nuclear War: Technology, Doctrine and Repercussions." *Yearbook of Finnish Foreign Policy*

1980. Helsinki: The Finnish Institute of International Affairs, 1980: 12–24.

Kelleher, Catherine McArdle. "The Present as Prologue: Europe and Theater Nuclear Force Modernization." *International Security.* Spring 1981: 150–168.

Kissinger, Henry A. *Nuclear Weapons and Foreign Policy.* New York: Harper and Row, 1957.

Labrie, Roger P., and Pranger, Robert J. *Nuclear Strategy and National Security: Points-of-View.* Washington, D.C.: American Enterprise Institute for Public Policy Research, 1977.

Makins, Christoper K. "The TNF Modernization and 'Countervail:ng' Strategy." *Survival.* July/August 1981: 157–164.

McKinney, William R. "Tactical Nuclear Weapons: The Practical." *Military Review.* October 1981: 22–27.

Menaul, S.W.B. "The Use of Nuclear Weapons in the European Theater." *NATO's Fifteen Nations.* April/May 1975: 15–21.

Milton, T.R. "The Mystique of NATO's Nukes." *NATO Review.* January 1975: 26–31.

Nailor, Peter, and Alford, Johnathan. *The Future of Briatin's Deterrent Force.* Adelphi Paper No. 156. London: International Institute for Strategic Studies, 1980.

Nerlich, Uwe. "Theater Nuclear Forces in Europe: Is NATO Running Out of Options?" *The Washington Quarterly.* Winter, 1980: 100–125.

Nott, John. "Nuclear Weapons and Preventing War." *NATO Review.* June 1981: 24–26.

Quinlan, James A. *Viability of a Tactical Nuclear Defense for NATO.* Carlisle, Pa.: U.S. Army War College, October 1977.

Record, Jeffrey. *NATO's Theater Nuclear Force Modernization: The Real Issues.* Washington D.C.: Institute for Foreign Policy Analysis, Inc., 1981.

Richardson, Robert C. "NATO Nuclear Strategy: A Look Back." *Strategic Review.* Spring 1981: 35–43.

Schelling, T.C. "Nuclear Strategy in Europe.," *World Politics.* April 1962: 4–21.

Starry, General Donn A. "Extending the Battlefield." *Military Review.* March 1981: 31–50.

Stockholm International Peace Research Institute. *Tactical Nuclear Weapons: European Perspectives.* London: Taylor and Francis, Ltd., 1978.

"Theater Nuclear Force Modernization." *RUSI Journal.* September 1980: 3–10, 37–43. (Report of a Seminar held at the RUSI in conjunction with the British Atlantic Committee on February 12, 1980: Dr. G.F. Treverton, Dr. L. Freedman, Mr. E. Griffiths, and Brigadier K. Hunt.)

Treverton, Gregory. *Nuclear Weapons in Europe.* Adelphi Paper No. 168. London: International Institute for Strategic Studies, Summer 1981.

"U.K./NATO Nuclear Options of the 1980s." *International Defense Review.* no. 9, 1979: 1487–1488.
U.S. Congressional Budget Office. *Planning U.S. General Purpose Forces: The Theater Nuclear Forces.* Budget Issue Paper. Washington, D.C.: U.S. Congressional Budget Office, January 1977.
U.S. Congress. Senate. Committee on Foreign Relations. Subcommittee on U.S. Security Agreements and Commitments Abroad. *Nuclear Weapons and Foreign Policy.* Washington, D.C.: U.S. Government Printing Office, March 1974.
U.S. Congress. House of Representatives. Committee on Foreign Affairs. Subcommittee on Europe and the Middle East. *The Modernization of NATO's Long-Range Theater Nuclear Forces.* Prepared by the U.S. Library of Congress, Foreign Affairs and National Defense Division, Washington D.C.: U.S. Government Printing Office, 1981.
Van Cleave, William, and Cohen, S.T. *Tactical Nuclear Weapons: An Examination of the Issues.* New York: Crane, Russak, 1978.

Soviet Policy and Strategy

Douglass, Joseph D., and Hoeber, Amoretta M. "The Nuclear Warfighting Dimension of the Soviet Threat to Europe." *The Journal of Social and Political Studies.* Summer 1978.
_____. *Soviet Strategy for Nuclear War.* Stanford, Calif.: Hoover Institution Press, 1979.
Douglass, Joseph D. *Soviet Military Strategy in Europe.* New York: Pergamon Press, 1980.
_____. "Soviet Nuclear Strategy in Europe: A Selective Targeting Doctrine?" *Strategic Review.* Fall 1980.
_____. *The Soviet Theater Nuclear Offensive.* Washington, D.C.: U.S. Government Printing Office, 1976.
Frank, Lewis Allen. *Soviet Nuclear Planning.* Washington, D.C.: American Enterprise Institute, 1977.
Garthoff, Raymond L. *Soviet Strategy in the Nuclear Age.* New York: Praeger Publishers, 1958.
Goure, Leon; Foy, D., and Harvey, Moxe L. *The Role of Nuclear Forces in Current Soviet Strategy.* Miami, Fla.: Center for Advanced International Studies, 1974.
Gromley, Dennis M. "Understanding Soviet Motivations for Deploying Long-Range Theater Nuclear Forces." *Military Review.* September 1981: 20–34.
Hyland, William G. "Soviet Theater Forces and Arms Control Policy." *Survival.* September/October 1981: 194–199.

Jones, Christopher. "The Soviet View of INF." *Arms Control Today*. March 1982: 4–5, 10.

Kennedy, Floyd D. "Theater Nuclear Encirclement: Soviet SLBMs Targeted on Western Europe." *National Defense,* February 1980.

MccGwire, Michael. "Soviet Military Doctrine: Contingency Planning and the Reality of World War." *Survival.* May/June 1980: 107–113.

Papp, Daniel S. "Nuclear Weapons and the Soviet Worldview." In *Soviet Armed Forces Review Annual 1980,* David R. Jones, ed., Gulf Breeze, Fla.: Academic International Press, 1980: 337–351.

Peterson, Philip A. "Flexibility: A Driving Force in Soviet Strategy." *Air Force.* March 1980: 94–98.

Savkin, V.Y. "The Basic Principals of Operational Art and Tactics: A Soviet View" *Soviet Military Thought, No. 4.* Washington, D.C.: U.S. Government Printing Office, 1974.

Siderenko, A.A. "The Offensive: A Soviet View." *Soviet Military Thought, No. 1.* Washington, D.C.: U.S. Government Printing Office, 1974.

———. "Soviet Tactics on the Nuclear Battlefield." *Military Review.* June 1965: 78–90.

Snyder, Jack L. *The Soviet Strategic Culture: Implications for Limited Nuclear Operations.* Santa Monica, Calif.: Rand Corporation, 1977.

Soviet Reactions to U.S./NATO Force Modernization. Arlington, Va.: Strategic Studies Center, 1977.

The Threat to Europe. Moscow: Soviet Committee for European Security and Cooperation and Scientific Research Committee on Peace and Disarmament, November 1981.

U.S. Department of Defense. *Soviet Military Power.* Washington, D.C.: U.S. Government Printing Office, 1981.

The Balance of Forces

"The Balance of Theater Nuclear Forces in Europe." *Aerospace International.* 16: 136–138.

"The Balance of Theater Nuclear Forces in Europe." *Aviation Week and Space Technology.* December 1980: 125–127.

"The Balance of Theater Nuclear Forces in Europe." *The Military Balance, 1980–1981.* London: International Institute for Strategic Studies, 1980.

"The Balance of Theater Nuclear Forces in Europe." *The Military Balance, 1981–1982.* London: International Institute for Strategic Studies, 1981.

Cordesman, Anthony H. "Europe's Quiet Profile in Courage," *Armed Forces Journal International.* June 1981: 38–56, 108–109.

Gelb, Leslie H. "Questions and Answers on the Military Balance in Europe." *The New York Times.* April 11, 1982.

Hopkins, Mark. "Baffling the Arms Controllers: Our New Euromissiles and Theirs." *New Leader.* October 6, 1980: 6–8.

Moore, Robert. "Theater Nuclear Forces." *International Defense Review.* no. 4, 1981: 401–408.

Pond, Elizabeth. "The Real Euromissile Tally." *The Christian Science Monitor.* November 27, 1981.

Sharp, Jane M.O. "Four Approaches to an INF Agreement." *Arms Control Today.* March 1982: 1–3, 6–8.

Weapons Systems

Berry, F. Clifton, Jr. "Pershing II: First Step in NATO Theater Nuclear Force Modernization." *International Defense Review.* no. 8, 1979: 1303–1308.

Betts, Richard K. *Cruise Missiles: Technology, Strategy, Politics.* Washington, D.C.: The Brookings Institution, 1981.

Blacker, Coit Dennis, and Hussain, Farooq. "European Theater Nuclear Forces." *The Bulletin of Atomic Scientists.* October, 1980: 32–37.

Daggett, Stephen. *The New Generation of Nuclear Weapons.* Washington, D.C.: Institute for Policy Studies, 1980.

Lautenschlager, Karl. "Theater Nuclear Forces and Grey Area Weapons." *The Naval War College Review.* September/October 1980: 13–22.

Lewis, Kevin N. "Intermediate-Range Nuclear Weapons." *Scientific American.* December 1980: 63–73.

Moore, Robert. "Theater Nuclear Forces." *International Defense Review.* no. 4, 1981: 401–408.

Morgenstern, John. "C^3 for Tactical Nuclear Forces in Europe." *Signal.* December 1980: 57–58.

Paine, Christopher. "Pershing II: The Army's Strategic Weapon." *The Bulletin of the Atomic Scientists,* October 1980: 25–31.

Record, Jeffrey. *U.S. Nuclear Weapons in Europe.* Washington, D.C.: The Brookings Institution, 1974.

Stockholm International Peace Research Institute. "Eurostrategic Weapons." *World Armaments and Disarmament. SIPRI Yearbook 1980.* London: Taylor and Francis, 1980:175–186.

U.S. General Accounting Office. *Most Critical Testing Still Lies Ahead for Missiles in Theater Nuclear Modernization.* Washington, D.C.: U.S. Government Printing Office, 1981.

Wrenn, Henry. *Cruise Missiles.* U.S. Library of Congress, Foreign Affairs and National Defense Division. Washington, D.C.: U.S. Government Printing Office, 1981.

The Neutron Weapon

Brauch, Hans Gunther. "The Enhanced Radiation Warhead: A West German Perspective." *Arms Control Today.* June 1978: 1–4.

Collins, Arthur S., Jr. "View from the Fourth Estate: The Neutron Weapon: Is it Right for Europe?" *Parameters.* December 1981: 80–83.

———. "The Enhanced Radiation Warhead: A Military Perspective." *Arms Control Today.* June 1978: 1–5.

Gans, Daniel. "Neutron Weapons: Solution to a Surprise Attack?" *Military Review.* February 1982: 55–73.

Kaplan, Fred M. "Enhanced Radiation Weapons." *Scientific American.* May 1978: 44–51.

Kaplan, Herman, and Warnke, Paul C. "The Neutron Bomb: What It Is, The Way It Works." *The Bulletin of the Atomic Scientists.* October 1981: 6–7.

Luttwak, Edward. "Tactical Advance: The Rationality of the 'Neutron Bomb'." *The New Republic.* September 16, 1981: 12–13.

"Neutron Bomb: A Mistake in Political, Military and Geopolitical Planning." *Journal of the Federation of American Scientists,* October 1981: 3–7.

"Neutron Bomb: Reactions from Europe." *The Bulletin of the Atomic Scientists.* October 1981: 7–13, 59–60.

Scoville, Herbert, Jr. "The Neutron Bomb Makes Politics Not War." *The New York Times.* August 26, 1981.

Seifritz, W. "Is There Protection Against Neutron Weapons?" *International Defense Review.* 14: 1571–1572.

Shreffler, R.G. "The Neutron Bomb for NATO Defense: An Alternative." *Orbis.* Winter 1978: 959–973.

Sommer, Theo. "It's the Way the Decision Was Made." *The Washington Post.* August 17, 1981.

Weinberger, Casper W. "Why Neutron Weapons, Why Now?" *The Washington Post.* August 11, 1981.

Wisner, Kent F. "Military Aspects of Enhanced Radiation Weapons." *Survival.* November/December 1981: 245–251.

Wrenn, Henry. *Enhanced Radiation Weapons.* U.S. Library of Congress, Foreign Affairs and National Defense Division, Washington, D.C.: U.S. Government Printing Office, 1981.

Disarmament and European Neutralism

Ball, Robert. "Getting Our Friends to Flex Their Muscles." *Fortune.* February 9, 1981: 60–64.

Bolkestein, F. "The Netherlands and the Lure of Neutralism." *NATO Review.* October 1981: 1–6.

Bibliography

Broder, David S. "Fading Memories Threaten the West." *The Washington Post.* July 12, 1981.

Elliot, David C. *Decision at Brussels: The Politics of Nuclear Forces.* Discussion Paper No. 97. Santa Monica, Calif. The California Seminar on International and Foreign Policy, August 1981.

"European Nuclear Disarmament: An Appeal for ACTION." *Bulletin of Peace Proposals.* February 1980.

Evangelista, Matthew; Forsberg, Randall; and Niedergang, Mark. "END and a Nuclear Freeze." *Armament and Disarmament Information Unit Report.* July/August 1981: 4–6.

Freedman, Lawrence. "A Criticism of the European Nuclear Disarmament Movement." *Armament and Disarmament Information Unit Report.* October/November 1980.

──────. "Britain: The First Ex-Nuclear Power?" *International Security.* Fall 1981: 80–104.

Galen, Justin. "Theater Nuclear Weapons and the Crisis in Europe's Leadership." *Armed Forces Journal International.* November 1981: 42–48.

Greider, William. "Let's Tell Our Allies Uncle Sucker is Dead." *The Washington Post.* July 12, 1981.

Hoffman, Stanley. "The Western Alliance: Drift on Harmony?" *International Security.* Fall 1981: 105–125.

Jenkins, Peter. "We Must Re-educate People in the Merits of Deterrence." *The Manchester Guardian.* November 8, 1981.

Kaldor, Mary. "END Can Be a Beginning." *The Bulletin of the Atomic Scientists.* December 1981: 42–46.

Kaplan, Fred. "Nuclear Showdown in Europe." *Inquiry.* May 25, 1981: 10–12.

Kondracke, Morton. "Nuclear Innocents Abroad." *The New Republic.* May 9, 1981: 16–18.

Laqueur, Walter. "Euro-Neutralism." *Commentary.* June 1980: 21–27.

──────. "Hollanditis: A New Stage in European Neutralism." *Commentary.* August 1981: 19–26.

Lucas, Michael. "The END of the Beginning." *The Nation.* October 10, 1981: 336–339.

"Multi-National Stand-Off Missile Development?" *International Defense Review.* no. 8, 1981: 978–979.

Ruhel, Hans. "The Theater Nuclear Issue in German Politics." *Strategic Review.* Spring 1981: 54–60.

Steel, Ronald. "A Neutral Europe?" *The New Republic.* November 11, 1981: 19–22.

Stone, Jeremy. "European Disarmament Movement Really Wants Unilateral Disarmament." *Journal of the Federation of American Scientists.* December 1981: 1–16.

Thompson, E.P., and Smith, Dan. *Protest and Survive.* New York: Monthly Review Press, 1981.
Whittle, Peter. "The Committee on Disarmament." *Armament and Disarmament Information Unit Report.* September/October 1981: 11–13.
Worner, Manfred. "The Peace Movement and NATO: An Alternative View from Bonn." *Strategic Review.* Winter 1982: 15–21.
Young, Elizabeth. "END and Politics in Europe." *Armament and Disarmament Information Unit Report.* May/June 1981: 16–18.

Index

Afghanistan, 41, 85
Aircraft, treatment in negotiations, 90–91
Anti-Americanism, 42, 46
Anti-nuclear movement, xviii, 42
Arms Control Association, xix
Assault Breaker, 58
Atlantic Alliance, 103–108; and arms 21–37; and NATO modernization plan, 46–47; weaknesses, 57
Atomic demolition mines (ADMS), 75

Backfire bombers, 2, 3, 10, 18, 19, 67, 74, 90, 91, 92f
Badger bombers, 71, 74
Battlefield nuclear weapons, 16–17, 58–59
Belgium, TNF modernization, 44
Berlin, Quadripartite Agreement on, 103
Biden, Joseph R., 55
Big Four, 61, 62
Blinder bombers, 74
Bombers, manned, 66, 71
Brandt, Willy, 106
Brezhnev, Leonid, xix, xx, 73, 87, 132; *Spiegel* interview, 95
Brown, Harold, 24, 25, 72
Brussels, NATO meeting in, 1979, 131–133
Buccaneer bombers, 66, 71
Burt, Richard, xiv, xvi, 1, 109–119

C^3, 33, 34
Carter administration, xvii, 41, 53
Carter, Jimmy, 24, 25–26, 61
Central America, U.S. policies in, 46, 52
Central Europe, 14–17
Chemical weapons, 16
China: IRBM, 71; Soviet forces oriented toward, 93
Christian Democrats, Netherlands, 44
Chronology, 121–130

Comprehensive approach, negotiating, 75–77
Corterier, Peter, xvi, xvii, xviii, 1, 103–108
Coupling, 59–60, 143
Cruise missiles. *See* GLCMs; Sea-launched cruise missiles
Cuba, U.S. relations with, 46

DDR. *See* German Democratic Republic
Defense planning, 66–67
DeGaulle, Charles, 22, 23, 40
Detente, 41, 54
DeVries, Klaas G., xv, xviii, xix, 51–64
Disarmament Commission, NYC, 138

East Germany, 15. *See also* German Democratic Republic
EEC. *See* European Economic Community
El Salvador, 44
Enhanced-radiation warheads (ERW), 17, 144
Erhard, Ludwig, 23
European Economic Community (EEC), veto of British application to, 22
European Nuclear Disarmament (END) campaign, 44, 72
Expansionism, Soviet, 41

F-4 bombers, 76, 144
F-104 Starfighter, 31
F-111 bombers, 3, 31, 90, 144
FBS, 65
Fitter aircraft, 76
Foot, Michael, 44
Ford, Gerald, 24, 54
France: IRBM, 71; nuclear forces, 61, 92–93
Free Democratic Party, West Germany, 44
Freedman, Lawrence, 74

161

Freeze movement, U.S., 29
Frog missiles, 75, 76
Functionally related observable differences (FRODs), 72

Geneva talks, 1981, 60, 61, 67–68, 71–72, 73, 75, 76, 85–102
Genscher, Herr, 106
German Democratic Republic, Basic Treaty with, 103
GLCMs, xviii, 2, 8, 10, 24, 34, 39, 58–59, 60, 72, 74, 75, 86, 89, 91, 95, 115f, 144; range limit, 24–25
Great Britain: IRBM, 71; nuclear forces, 61, 92–93; TNF modernization, 44
Gromyko, Foreign Minister, 73
Ground-launched continental missiles. See GLCMs
Guadaloupe, Big Four meeting in, 1979, 61

Haig, Alexander, 29, 52, 54, 73, 104, 105, 107, 118
Harmel Report, xviii, 53–54, 55, 104
High Level Group, NATO, 85, 118, 144
Honest John missile, 75, 144
Hyland, William, 74

ICBMs (Intercontinental ballistic missiles), xv, 81
INF (Intermediate nuclear force), 59, 60, 81–102, 144; and arms control, 26–35; modernization, 21, 23–26, 41, 45, 117
IRBMs (intermediate-range ballistic missiles), xv, 40, 69, 71, 81, 113, 145
Italy, TNF modernization, 44

Joffe, Joseph, xvii, xviii, xix, 21–37
Jupiter missile, xv, xvi, xvii, 67, 76, 81

Kennedy administration, 22
Kissinger, Henry, 21, 57
Krefeld Appeal, 1981, xviii

Labour Party, Great Britain, 44
Lance missile, 17, 75, 145

Launchers, as unit of parity account, 89–90
Leber, Georg, 25
Limited-conventional warfare, 14
Limited nuclear exchange, 59
Long-range theater nuclear forces. See LRTNF
LRTNF, 11, 18–19, 24, 25, 27, 29, 31, 33, 39–48, 87–94; military dimensions, 2–6; modernization program, 40, 44–48, 60, 68; political dimensions, 6–7
Luns, Secretary-General, 2

Mace, 67, 76
MacNamara, Robert, 76
Madrid, 1980 CSCE meeting in, 136–137
Matador, 67, 76
MBFR. See Mutual and Balanced Force Reduction Medium-range nuclear-capable bombers, 71
Mutual and Balanced Force Reduction (MBFR) talks, Vienna, 65, 87, 98, 138, 145
"Mixed Option," 8
Military Balance 1981/82, 31
Mirage IV, 31
MLF (multilateral force), xvii, 21–23, 26, 86, 145
MRBM (medium-range ballistic missile), 21, 145
Multilateral Force. See MLF
MX-missile program, 47, 77

Nachrustung, 26
NATO (North Atlantic Treaty Organization): arms conference, 1981, 1, 1–11; arms control, xix–xx, 56–58; communique, 12/12/79, 131–133; communique, 12/14/79, 135–141; dual decision, 1979, xvi, xvii, 8–9, 59–60, 61–63, 103–108; High Level Group, 85, 118, 144; nuclear deterrence, 109–119; Nuclear Planning Group, 61; Option III

Index

proposal, 76; Special Consultative Group, 85, 118, 146
Negotiations, 1–11, 81–102; approaches, 68–77
Nerlich, Uwe, 24
Netherlands, opposition to TNF modernization, 44
Neutralism, Europe, 42
Neutron bomb, 25, 75
NFZs. *See* Nuclear free zones
Nightingale, Florence, 118
Nike Hercules, 76, 77
Non-Proliferation Treaty (NPT), 23, 65
Norstad, General, 103
North Atlantic Assembly, 62
North Atlantic Treaty Organization. *See* NATO
Nuclear balance, Europe, 65–68; U.S. and USSR view of, 68
Nuclear free zones (NFZs), 72
Nuclear Planning Group (NPG), NATO, 24, 61, 132, 145

Option III proposal, NATO, 76
Ostpolitik, 106

Parity, 1–2, 39–40, 60; based on launchers or warheads, 89–90
Peace movement, Europe, 29, 42
Pershing I, 3, 32f, 74
Pershing IA, 74, 76
Pershing II, xvii, xviii, xix, 2, 8, 10, 28f, 32f, 34, 39, 60, 74, 85, 86, 89, 95, 109, 115f, 116, 145–146
Pershing IIA, 58, 145
Pierre, Andrew, xvi–xvii, 39–48
Pluton, 75
Poland, 41, 61, 88; and START, 73
Polaris missiles, xv, 22, 66, 67
Poseidon, xx, 67, 146

Quadripartite Agreement, Berlin, 103

Reagan administration, 41, 53; and arms control, 45, 56, 61, 85; and SALT II, xviii–xix, 77, 88
Reagan, Ronald, xix, xx, 73, 77; and arms control, 85; zero option, 29–30, 31, 33, 47, 73, 96
Rhodesia, 139
Richardson, Elliot L., 1–11
Rosow, Eugene, 54

SAC. *See* Strategic Air Command
SACEUR. *See* Supreme Allied Commander Europe
SALT (strategic arms limitation talks), 146
SALT I, 90
SALT II, xviii–xix, 2, 24–26, 41, 55, 60, 67, 73–74, 77, 85, 87–89, 136
SALT III, 60, 140
SAM-2s, 76
Scaleboard missile, 75, 76
Schlesinger, James, 24, 33
Schmidt, Helmut, 44, 73, 114; 1977 speech, International Institute for Strategic Studies, xvi, xvii, 3, 24–25, 26, 40, 85
Scud missile, 75, 76
Sea-launched cruise missiles, 47–48, 75, 146
SALT-plus approach, negotiating, 73–75
Selin, Ivan, 2, 13–19
Sharp, Jane, xv, xxi, 65–79
Short-range nuclear-capable strike aircraft, 69
Simonet Henri, 1–11
SLBM warheads, 93
Social Democratic Party, West Germany, xviii, 26–27, 44
Special Consultative Group, NATO, 7, 10, 85, 118
Spiegel, Der, Brezhnev interview, 1981, 94
SS-4, xv, xvi, 21, 22, 23, 29, 33, 73, 82f, 113, 146
SS-5, xv, xvi, 21, 22, 23, 29, 33, 73, 83f, 113, 146
SS-11, 67
SS-17, 88
SS-18, 88
SS-19, 67, 88
SS-12, 91

SS-20, xvi, xvii, 2, 3, 8, 10, 18, 19, 33, 34, 40, 59, 60, 71, 73, 76, 84f, 86, 88, 91, 93, 94, 95, 97-98, 110, 114, 147; and SALT II, 67
SS-21, 76, 91, 97–98
SS-22, 76, 91, 97–98
SS-23, 91, 97–98
SSBS S-2 missile, 86
START (strategic-arms-reduction talks), xxi, 73, 77, 85–89
Strategic Air Command (SAC), 22–23
Strategic-arms-reduction talks, *See* START
Status-quo-ante approach, negotiating, 72–77
Status-quo approach, negotiating, 70–72
Supreme Allied Commander Europe (SACEUR), xx, 146

Tactical nuclear-delivery vehicles, 70
Thatcher government, Great Britain, 44
Theater-nuclear-arms control, 117–119
Third country nuclear forces, 92–93

Thompson, E.P., 44
Thor missile, xv, xvi, xvii, 67, 76, 81
Titan missile, 76
TNF, 147; shorter-range, 91–92; *See See also* LRTNF
Tomahawk, 39
Treverton, Gregory, xv, xxi, 81–102
Trident I, 44

Vance, Cyrus, 57
Verification, 93–94
Vienna, MBFR negotiations in, 76, 87, 98
Vietnam war, 52
Vulcan bomber, 3, 31, 66, 71

Warheads, as unit of parity account, 89–90
Weinberger, Caspar, 29
West Germany, xvii, xviii, 15; MLF and, 22, 23; and NATO dual decision, 43–44

Zero option, 8, 29, 31, 33, 47, 73, 96

About the Contributors

Richard Burt is the U.S. assistant secretary of state designate, Bureau of European Affairs. Since January 1981, Mr. Burt has been serving as director of the Bureau of Politico-Military Affairs at the Department of State. Previously, he was the National Security Affairs Correspondent for *The New York Times,* covering foreign-policy and defense issues in Washington. Mr. Burt has served as assistant director of the International Institute for Strategic Studies, London; was a research associate at the International Institute for Strategic Studies; worked as an advanced-research fellow at the U.S. Naval War College, Newport, Rhode Island; and was an advisor on defense and arms control to the House Representatives Republican Wednesday Group.

Peter Corterier is a Staats minister of the Federal Republic of Germany. Dr. Corterier studied law, economics, and political science at the Universities of Heidelberg, Freiburg, and Bonn. He has been a member of the Social Democratic Party since 1956 and became the youngest member of its executive committee in 1965. Dr. Corterier has been a representative to the West German parliament since 1969. Other posts he has held include: president of the Atlantic Association of Young Political Leaders, 1965–1968; vice-president of the North Atlantic Assembly, 1977–1979; and membership in the European Parliament, 1973–1977.

Klaas G. de Vries has been a representative in the Dutch Parliament since 1973. He is a member of the Dutch Labor Party and serves as its secretary in Parliament. Specializing in defense and foreign affairs, Dr. de Vries chaired the Standing Committee on Defense until September 1981. In addition, Dr. de Vries is a member of the Labor Party Committee on the Middle East, cochairman of the Association for Euro-Arab Cooperation, and a delegate to the North Atlantic Assembly. Dr. de Vries received the degree in Dutch Law from the University of Utrecht in 1968.

Josef Joffe is a senior editor of the German weekly publication *Die Zeit.* He received the B.A. from Swarthmore College, the M.A. from Johns Hopkins University, and the Ph.D. from Harvard University. He has contributed to *Foreign Affairs, Foreign Policy, Survival* and **Europa-Archiv,** as well as to various books dealing with German foreign policy, international politics, and strategy. He is a member of the International Institute of Strategic Studies in London.

Andrew J. Pierre is a senior Fellow at the Council on Foreign Relations where he has also been acting director of studies. Formerly on the staffs of the Brookings Institution and the Hudson Institute, he has also taught at Columbia University. From 1962 to 1964 he was the Department of State, first in Washington, and later at the American embassy in London, and he is a consultant to several government agencies. His most recent book is *The Global Politics of Arms Sales.* He has published articles in such journals as *Foreign Affairs, Foreign Policy, Survival,* and *International Security.*

Elliot L. Richardson has led a distinguished and varied career in government service. His posts have included secretary of Health, Education and Welfare; secretary of Defense; attorney general; secretary of Commerce; and ambassador to the Court of St. James. Ambassador Richardson also served as the Special Representative of the President to the Law-of-the-Sea Conference. He now practices law in Washington, D.C., and is chairman of the United Nations Association of the United States.

Henri Simonet has been in Belgian politics and government for fifteen years. He has held a variety of high governmental positions, including Secretary of State for Economic Affairs and, most recently, Minister of Foreign Affairs from 1977–1980. Mr. Simonet has published books and articles on economics, finance, and politics. Currently he is a professor at the University Libre de Bruxelles.

Ivan Selin is the founder and chairman of the board of American Management Systems, Inc., a consulting and computer-services firm. For the five years prior to his founding the company in 1970, Dr. Selin served in the Department of Defense, eventually becoming acting assistant secretary for Systems Analysis. From 1960 until 1965, he was at the RAND Corporation in Santa Monica, California, where he studied statistical decision theory. Dr. Selin is an active member in the United Nation Association of the United States and has been a member of the Council on Foreign Relations since 1979. He received the B.S., M.S., and Ph.D. degrees from Yale University.

Jane M.O. Sharp is currently a visiting scholar at the Peace Studies Program at Cornell University, where she is directing the project on the Warsaw Pact. She was formerly a research associate at the Harvard University Center for Science and International Affairs. Ms. Sharp is a board member of the Council for a Livable World and is active in the International Pugwash Movement. She is the editor of *Opportunities for Disarmament* and author of numerous articles on European-security issues.

Gerard C. Smith is a principal of the Consultants International Group; a limited partner with Alex, Brown and Sons, investment bankers; and a director of the Panhandle Eastern Pipeline Company. From 1977–1980, Mr. Smith was ambassador-at-large and presidential special representative for nonproliferation. In 1981, he was awarded the Presidential Medal of Freedom, the nation's highest civilian award. From 1973–1977, Mr. Smith held a variety of posts, among them trustee of Catholic University and the Brookings Institution. He was also a member of the advisory boards to The Johns Hopkins University School for Advanced International Studies and the Committee on Arms Control and Disarmament. In 1973, he received the Medal of Merit from Yale Univeristy Law School. In the three years prior to 1973, Mr. Smith was director of the Arms Control and Disarmament Agency and chief of the SALT I delegation. His book, *Doubletalk, The Story of SALT I,* was published in 1980.

Gregory F. Treverton is a lecturer in public policy at the Kennedy School of Government, Harvard University. Dr. Treverton was previously assistant director at the International Institute for Strategic Studies in London as well as a staff member for West European studies at the National Security Council. He received the B.A. in public and international affairs from Princeton Univeristy, and the Master of Public Policy and Ph.D. degrees from Harvard University. He is the author and editor of numerous articles, reports, and books.

About the Editors

Marsha McGraw Olive was appointed associate director of the Arms Control Association in 1980. She previously served in the Non-Proliferation Bureau of the Arms Control and Disarmament Agency as the desk officer for Soviet and East European affairs and U.S. nuclear-export policy. From 1975 to 1977 she was chief legislative assistant to a U.S. congressman. Educated at Duke University and The Johns Hopkins School of Advanced International Studies, she also attended the University of Moscow and the Institute of Politics and Economics in Belgrade, Yugoslavia. She is a member of the Committee on Future Dutch-American Relations and a contributor to various newspapers and periodicals.

Jeffrey D. Porro has been the editor of *Arms Control Today* since April 1980. He previously served as a politico-military-affairs officer with the State Department's Bureau of Politico-Military Affairs (1978-1979). Before that he was legislative assistant for foreign affairs and armed services with Senator Howard Metzenbaum. He has written articles published in *Arms Control Today* and *The Bulletin of the Atomic Scientists*. He received the Ph.D. in political science from the University of California at Los Angeles.